CELEBRITY ALIASES UNMASKED!

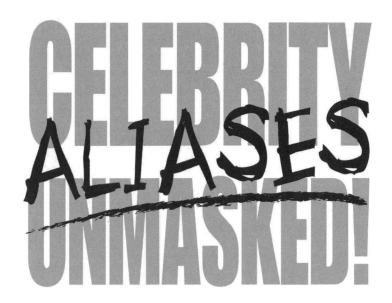

CELEBRITY ALIASES UNMASKED!

Jake Beasley

SWEET WATER PRESS

CONTENTS

What's in a Name?

> "What's in a name? that which we call a rose
> By any other name would smell as sweet;
> So Romeo would, were he not Romeo call'd,
> Retain that dear perfection which he owes
> Without that title. Romeo, doff thy name,
> And for that name which is no part of thee
> Take all myself."
> —Shakespeare, from *Romeo and Juliet*

What is in a name? A lot, if this example by Shakespeare is any indication. In this famous story, a name was the one thing that kept Romeo and Juliet apart. If Romeo had only had the option of changing his name as many people do today!

When people change their name, we say that they have assumed an alias, which means "otherwise called" or "otherwise known as." The general term that covers this is "pseudonym." People take on a pseudonym for a variety of reasons. Sometimes they think their real name is not glamorous or exciting enough to suit them, it is embarrassing or can be made fun of too easily, or it reflects the wrong image. For these reasons and more, they change their name to more accurately reflect their lifestyle. Sometimes these changes are made legally, and sometimes not. Often people continue to use their birth name in some situations, and their pseudonym in others.

Many times, people change their names for professional reasons. For example, in past decades, actors often used stage names when they thought that their real names were too "ethnic." There are practical considerations too: Britain's actors' union and the Screen Actors Guild in the U.S. stipulate that no two members may have the same working name, so actors are often forced to modify their name or take a new one to avoid duplication. Actors may occasionally want to avoid being recognized, but since they generally seek attention rather than avoid it, they often use a pseudonym to create a persona of their own design.

Writers also often choose to work under a new name, called a pen name or *nom de plume*. In France, this is more commonly called a *nom de guerre*, or "name of war." Their reasons are numerous. Although anonymity is not usually one of those, because they can already be "invisible" if they choose to be, they may prefer a new name in order to write as a different gender. In earlier times, women writers very often disguised themselves as men simply to get published. In our modern society, writers may choose a different gender when a particular subject matter might not be accepted if presented from the "wrong" gender, such as *Memoirs of a Geisha* and *She's Come Undone*, both written by men from the perspective of a female.

Authors also use pen names to disguise their age or ethnicity, and to break into another genre. Would you be inclined to buy a romance novel by Stephen King? If an author has a large number of books to his or her credit, some of them may be published under a different name so that readers will not think the writer is just churning out books without taking proper time with each one. According to *Writer's Digest*, pen names are also used to provide a common identity when several people are writing together, and by writers trying to hide writing from their boss while they "hold on to their day job."

There are as many reasons for changing one's name as there are people who change them. We are familiar with some stories of famous people and why they have changed their names. Others are more obscure. Our book offers a collection of both. And no doubt it includes those we would not know about at all if they had not changed their name.

ACTORS,
ACTRESSES,
&
PERFORMERS

ACTORS, ACTRESSES, & PERFORMERS

ALIAS (REAL NAME)

Alan Alda (Alphonso Joseph D'Abruzzo)

Played Hawkeye in $M*A*S*H*$ and has starred in many movies and TV series.

Jason Alexander (Jason Scott Greenspan)

Played George on *Seinfeld*.

Tim Allen (Tim Allen Dick)

Actor and comedian.

Woody Allen (Allen Stewart Konigsberg)

Actor, writer, and director of movies and plays, including *Annie Hall* and *Hannah and Her Sisters*.

Kirstie Alley (Gladys Leeman)

Actress. Played on *Cheers* and starred in many movies.

> In the movie *Drop Dead Gorgeous*, **Kirstie Alley** played a character by the name of Gladys Leeman, which is her real name.

Don Ameche (Dominic Felix Amici)

Actor, starred in *Cocoon*.

Julie Andrews (Julia Elizabeth Wells)

Actress, starred in *The Sound of Music*.

Jennifer Aniston (Jennifer Linn Anastassakis)

Actress. Played Rachel on hit TV series *Friends*.

Desi Arnaz (Desiderio Alberto Arnaz y de Acha III)

Bandleader and co-star of *I Love Lucy*.

Desiderio Alberto Arnaz y de Acha III arrived in the United States with his family in the 1930s. To earn a living for the family, he shortened his name to Desi Arnaz.

Rosanna Arquette (Rosanna Lauren)

Actress, starred in *Desperately Seeking Susan* and *Pulp Fiction*.

Bea Arthur (Bernice Frankel)

Actress and comedian. Starred in *Maude* and *The Golden Girls*.

Fred Astaire (Frederick Austerlitz)

Actor and dancer, starred in *Top Hat*.

Frankie Avalon (Francis Thomas Avallone)

Actor and singer. Best known for 1960s beach movies.

Charles Aznavour (Shahnour Aznavurjan)

French actor, singer, and composer.

Lauren Bacall (Betty Joan Perske)

Actress best known for *Murder on The Orient Express* and *The Shootist*.

Catherine Bach (Catherine Bachman)
Played Daisy Duke in *The Dukes of Hazzard.*

Lucille Ball (Dianne Belmont)
Comedian, actress, and star of *I Love Lucy.* Wife of Desi Arnaz.

Anne Bancroft (Anna Maria Luisa Italiano)
Starred in *The Graduate* and *Miracle Worker.*

Lionel Barrymore (Lionel Herbert Blythe)
Famous stage actor. Grandfather of Drew Barrymore.

Warren Beatty (Henry Warren Beaty)
Actor and director. Played in *Bonnie and Clyde* and *Dick Tracy.*

Bonnie Bedelia (Bonnie Culkin)
Actress. Played in *Die Hard* and *Die Hard 2.*

Dirk Benedict (Dirk Niewoehner)
Played Face in *The A-Team* and Starbuck on *Battlestar Galactica.*

Jack Benny (Benjamin Kubelsky)
Actor and comedian. Had his own TV show.

Tom Berenger (Thomas Michael Moore)
Actor. Played in *Major League* and *Platoon*, as well as many other movies and TV shows.

Busby Berkeley (William Berkeley Enos)
Choreographer for musicals such as *Annie Get Your Gun.*

Milton Berle (Milton Berlinger)
Comedian.

Robert Blake (Michael Gubitosi)
Starred in *Beretta*.

Shirley Booth (Thelma Marjorie Ford)
Actress. Played Hazel on the TV series.

Ernest Borgnine (Ermes Effron Borgnino)
Actor. *The Wild Bunch* and *The Dirty Dozen*.

Pierre Brasseur (Pierre-Albert Espinasse)
Starred in *King of Hearts*.

Morgan Brittany (Suzanne Cupito)
Actress. Played Baby June in *Gypsy*.

Charles Bronson (Charles Buchinski)
Actor. Played in *Death Wish* and *Once Upon a Time in the West*.

> With the change of a few letters in his last name, **Charles Buchinski** became Charles Bronson.

Albert Brooks (Albert Einstein)
Actor and director of many movies, including *Broadcast News*.

Mel Brooks (Melvin Kaminsky)
Actor and director of many movies, including *Blazing Saddles*.

Lenny Bruce (Leonard Alfred Schneider)
Cutting edge comedian and satirist.

Yul Brynner (Taidje Kahn)

Actor. Played in *The King and I*, *Westworld*, and *The Magnificent Seven*.

George Burns (Nathanial Birnbaum)

Actor and comedian; played in *Oh God!*

Ellen Burstyn (Edna Gilhooley)

Actress. Played in *Alice Doesn't Live Here Anymore*.

Richard Burton (Richard Walter Jenkins Jr.)

Actor. Played in *Who's Afraid of Virginia Woolf?*

Red Buttons (Aaron Chwatt)

Comedian.

Nicolas Cage (Nicolas Coppola)

Actor; nephew of Francis Ford Coppola.

Francis Ford Coppola's nephew, **Nicolas Cage**, changed his name so he wouldn't get any breaks based on the success of his uncle.

Michael Caine (Maurice J. Micklewhite)

Actor and producer.

Maria Callas (Maria Kalogeropoulos)

Opera star.

Dyan Cannon (Samile Diane Friesen)

Actress. Played in *Bob & Carol & Ted & Alice* and *Author! Author!*

Eddie Cantor (Edward Israel Iskowitz)

Radio and TV actor.

Kate Capshaw (Kathleen Sue Nail)

Actress. Played in *Indiana Jones and The Temple of Doom*. Married to Steven Spielberg.

Captain Kangaroo (Robert Keeshan)

Children's TV personality.

Capucine (Germaine Lefebvre)

Actress and model. Played Simone Clousea in *The Pink Panther*.

Tia Carrere (Althea Janairo)

Actress and singer. Played in *Wayne's World*.

Diahann Carroll (Carol Diahann Johnson)

Actress and singer. Played Julia in the television series.

Joanna Cassidy (Joanna Virginia Caskey)

Actress. Played Zhora in *Blade Runner*.

Phoebe Cates (Phoebe Katz)

Actress. Played in *Gremlins* and *Fast Times at Ridgemont High*.

Kim Cattrall (Clare Woodgate)

Played Samantha Jones on *Sex and the City*, and in *Porky's* and *Police Academy*.

Emma Caulfield (Emma Chukker)

Actress. Played in the TV series *Buffy the Vampire Slayer* and the movie *Darkness Falls*.

Cedric the Entertainer (Cedric Kyles)

Comedian. Played in *Barbershop*.

Jackie Chan (Chan Kong-Sang)

Actor famous for his martial arts movies.

Kelly Chan (Wai Man Chen)

Actress in many Hong Kong movies.

Stockard Channing (Susan Stockard)

Actress. Starred in *Grease*, and more recently in *The West Wing*.

Cyd Charisse (Tula Ellice Finklea)

Actress. A.k.a. Lily Norwood. Played in *Singin' In the Rain*.

Charo (Maria Rosario Pilar, Martinez Molina Baeza)

Flamenco guitarist and performer. Charo made numerous appearances on *The Love Boat*.

Chevy Chase (Cornelius Crane Chase)

Actor, comedian, and *SNL* vet. Played in *Caddyshack*, *Fletch*, National Lampoon's *Vacation* movies, and many others.

Chevy Chase's real first name is Cornelius. Chevy was actually a childhood name, reportedly given to him by his grandmother based on the Maryland suburb. He took it as his stage name, and as a news anchor on SNL made famous the line "Good Evening, I'm Chevy Chase, and you're not."

Joan Chen (Chong Chen)

Actress, director, producer, and writer. Played Josie Packard on *Twin Peaks*.

Chico (Leonard Marx)

Comedian; one of the Marx Brothers.

Andrew Dice Clay (Andrew Clay Silverstein)

Comedian and actor.

Lee J. Cobb (Lee Jacoby)

Actor. Played in *The Exorcist*.

Claudette Colbert (Lily Claudette)

Actress. Played in *It Happened One Night*.

Robbie Coltrane (Robin MacMillan)

Actor, writer, producer, and director. Played Rubeus Hagrid in *Harry Potter* movies and the lead role in *Cracker* TV series.

Chuck Connors (Kevin Joseph Connors)

Actor. Starred in many westerns, *Old Yeller*, *Soylent Green*, and the TV series *Dark Shadows*.

Mike Connors (Krekor Ohanian)

Actor, best known for TV series *Mannix*.

Gary Cooper (Frank James Cooper)

Actor. Starred in *High Noon* and *Sergeant York*.

David Copperfield (David Kotkin)

Magician.

Alex Cord (Alexander Viespi)

Actor. Played in *Stagecoach* and the TV shows *Ringo Kid* and *Airwolf*.

Lou Costello (Louis Francis Cristillo)

Actor. Part of comedy team Abbott and Costello.

Peter Coyote (Peter Cohon)

Actor. Played Keys in *E.T.* and appeared in *Jagged Edge*.

Joan Crawford (Lucille Le Sueur)

Actress. Starred in *What Ever Happened to Baby Jane?*

Michael Crawford (Michael Dumble-Smith)

Actor and writer. Played in *Hello Dolly*.

Bing Crosby (Harry Lillis Crosby)

Actor and singer who first rose to stardom in the 1930s.

Tom Cruise (Thomas Cruise Mapother IV)

Actor. Became a household name after singing and dancing in his underwear in *Risky Business*.

> Before dropping the last name Mapother, **Thomas (Tom) Cruise** attended a Franciscan seminary and aspired to become a Catholic priest.

Curly (Jerome Lester Horwitz)

One of the *Three Stooges*.

Tony Curtis (Bernard Schwartz)

Actor. Played in *Spartacus* and *Some Like It Hot*.

Michael Curtiz (Mano Kaminer)

Directed *Casablanca* and *White Christmas*.

Dame Edna (Barry Humphries)

Cross-dressing comedian and actress.

Vic Damone (Vito Farinola)

Actor. Played in *An Affair To Remember*.

Rodney Dangerfield (Jacob Cohen)

Actor and comedian; movies include *Caddyshack* and *Back To School*. Best known for his line "I get no respect."

Ted Danson (Edward Bridge Danson III)

Actor. Played Sam Malone on *Cheers*.

Tony Danza (Anthony Ladanza)

Actor. Played in *Taxi* and *Who's The Boss?*

Marion Davies (Marion Cecilia Douras)

Actor. Made many movies in the 1920s and 30s. Lived with William Randolph Hearst.

Bette Davis (Ruth Elizabeth Davis)

Actress. Played in *All About Eve* and *What Ever Happened To Baby Jane?*

Doris Day (Doris Mary Ann Von Kappelhoff)

Actress and singer.

James Dean (James Byron)

Actor. Starred in *Rebel Without a Cause*.

Delores Del Rio (Lolita Dolores Martinez Asunsolo Lopez Negrette)

Mexican Actress. Played in *The Devil's Playground*.

Rebecca DeMornay (Rebecca George)

Actress. Played in *Risky Business* and *The Hand That Rocks The Cradle*.

Catherine Deneuve (Catherine Dorleac)

French Actress.

Bo Derek (Mary Cathleen Collins)

Actress. Starred in *10*. Made corn-row braided hair hip with white girls all over the country.

Who would go to a movie starring **Mary Cathleen Collins**? Not many people, but they would to see Bo Derek!

John Derek (Derek Harris)

Director of *10* and husband of Bo Derek.

Susan Dey (Susan Smith)

Actress. Starred in *The Partridge Family* and *L.A. Law*.

Angie Dickinson (Angeline Brown)

Actress. Starred in the TV series *Police Woman* and many movies.

Vin Diesel (Mark Vincent)

Actor. Played in *The Fast and the Furious*.

Marlene Dietrich (Marie Magdelene Dietrich von Losch)

Actress. Played in *Morocco*.

Phyllis Diller (Phyllis Driver)

Comedian and actress.

Divine (Harris Glenn Milstead)

Actor. Cross-dressing actor who appeared in *Hairspray* and many other John Waters movies.

Diana Dors (Diana Fluck)

Actress. Once promoted as the "British Marilyn Monroe."

Kirk Douglas (Issur Danielovitch Demsky)

Actor. Played in *Spartacus* and *20,000 Leagues Under The Sea*.

Melvyn Douglas (Melvyn Edouard Hesselberg)

Actor. Won an Academy Award for Best Supporting Actor for roles in *Hud* and *Being There*.

Dr. Drew (David Drew Pinsky)

Host of radio and MTV program *Loveline*.

Margaret Dumont (Daisey Juliette Baker)

Actress. Appeared in seven Marx Brothers films.

Rocky Echevarria (Steven Bauer)

Originally Cuban actor who has played in a variety of movies and TV movies.

Barbara Eden (Barbara Huffman)

Actress. Best-loved for her role in *I Dream of Jeannie*.

Blake Edwards (William Blake McEdwards)

Director of the *Pink Panther* movies.

Carmen Electra (Tara Leigh Patrick)

Playboy model, actress, and *Baywatch* star.

Elvira (Cassandra Peterson)

A.k.a. Mistress of the Dark. She gained fame wearing dark, gothic, and cleavage-enhancing clothing as host of *Elvira's Movie Macabre*.

Linda Evans (Linda Evanstad)
Actress. Starred in *Dynasty*.

Evel Knievel (Robert Craig Knievel)
Daredevil and pop icon. Starred as himself in the movie *Viva Knievel!*

Kenny Everett (Maurice Cole)
Broadcaster and comedian.

Tom Ewell (S. Yewell Tompkins)
Actor. Played in *The Seven Year Itch*.

Douglas Fairbanks (Douglas Elton Ulman)
Actor. Played in *The Mark of Zorro* and *Robin Hood*.

Morgan Fairchild (Patsy Ann McClenny)
Actress. Played in *Falcon Crest*.

Adam Faith (Terence Nelhams-Wright)
British actor and 1960s pop star.

Jamie Farr (Jameel Joseph Farah)
Actor. Starred in *M*A*S*H** as Klinger.

Sally Field (Sally Mahoney)
Actress. Played in *Smokey and the Bandit*, *Forrest Gump*, *The Flying Nun*, *Gidget*, and many other TV shows and movies.

Gracie Fields (Grace Stansfield)
British comedian and actor.

W. C. Fields (William Claude Dukenfield)
Actor and comedian.

Peter Finch (William Mitchell)
Actor. Played in *Sunday Bloody Sunday* and *Network*.

Linda Fiorentino (Clorinda Fiorentino)
Actress. Played in *Men In Black*.

Glenn Ford (Gwyilyn Ford)
Actor. Played in *Blackboard Jungle* and *Cimarron*.

John Forsythe (John Lincoln Freund)
Actor. Played in *Dynasty*.

Jodie Foster (Alicia Christian Foster)
Actress. Since beginning her career at the age of two, she has been the Coppertone Girl and starred in many movies.

Michael J. Fox (Michael Andrew Fox)
Actor. Played in *Family Ties, Spin City*, and the *Back to the Future* movies.

Michael J. Fox was born Michael Andrew Fox, but adopted the "J" as homage to character actor Michael J. Pollard.

Jamie Foxx (Eric Bishop)
Actor and comedian. Appeared in *Any Given Sunday* and *In Living Color*.

Redd Foxx (John Elroy Sanford)
Comedian. Starred in *Sanford and Son*.

Ali G (Sacha Baron Cohen)
Actor and producer. HBO's *Da Ali G. Show*.

Jean Gabin (Jean-Alexis Moncorge)
French Actor.

Zsa Zsa Gabor (Sari Gabor)
Actress.

Greta Garbo (Greta Lovisa Gustafsson)
Actress.

Andy Garcia (Andres Arturo Garci-Menendez)
Actor. Played in the *Untouchables* and *The Godfather III*.

Vincent Gardenia (Vincente Scognamiglio)
Actor. Played in *Bang the Drum Slowly*.

Judy Garland (Frances Ethel Gumm)
Actress. Played Dorothy in *The Wizard of Oz*. She is the mother of Liza Minelli.

Judy Garland started out as Frances Gumm, performing with her two other sisters as The Gumm Sisters. Someone recommended they choose a less humorous name, and they settled on the Three Garlands. Frances chose the name Judy to go with it.

James Garner (James Scott Baumgarner)
Actor. Played in *The Rockford Files* and *Maverick*.

Mitzi Gaynor (Franceska Mitzi Gerber)
Actress. Played in *South Pacific*.

Ben Gazzara (Biago Anthony Gazzara)

Actor and director.

Lillian Gish (Lillian de Guiche)

Actress. *Duel In the Sun.*

Paulette Goddard (Pauline Marion Goddard Levy)

Actress. Played in *The Great Dictator.*

Whoopi Goldberg (Caryn Johnson)

Actress and comic. Played in *Ghost.*

Caryn Johnson first chose the name Whoopi Cushion as a joke. When her mother told her she'd never get any respect with that name, she changed it to Whoopi Goldberg. A nice respectable name...

Elliott Gould (Elliott Goldstein)

Actor. Played in the movie *M*A*S*H** and the TV series *Friends* as Ross and Monica's father.

Stewart Granger (James Leblanche Stewart)

Actor. Played in *King Solomon's Minds.*

Cary Grant (Archibald Leach)

Actor in the Hollywood Studio age.

In speaking of himself, **Cary Grant** said, "My family name is Leach. To which, at my christening, was added Archibald Alexander, with no opportunity for me to protest."

Rachel Grant (Rachel Louise Grant de Longueuil)

Actress and model. Bond girl in *Die Another Day.*

Peter Graves (Peter Aurness)

Actor. Played in *Mission Impossible* (TV) and *Airplane!*

Joel Grey (Joel Katz)

Actor. Played in *Cabaret*.

Robert Guillaume (Robert Peter Williams)

Actor. Played in *Benson* and the TV series *Soap*.

Alec Guinness (Alec Guinness de Cuffe)

Actor. Played in *Star Wars* and *The Bridge Over The River Kwai*.

Gummo (Milton Marx)

The fifth Marx brother, stopped performing with Groucho before the brothers made it big, but managed his famous brothers for many years.

Arsenio Hall (Chuckton Arthur Hall)

Actor and talk show host.

Jean Harlow (Harlean Carpentier)

Actress. Made six films with Clark Gable.

Rex Harrison (Reginald Carey)

Actor. Played in *My Fair Lady*.

Mary Hart (Mary Johanna Harum)

Actress. TV host on *Entertainment Tonight*.

Rita Hayworth (Margarita Carmen Cansino)

Actress. Played in *Gilda* and *The Lady From Shanghai*.

Tippi Hedron (Melanie Daniels)
Actress in Hitchcock thriller *The Birds*.

Benny Hill (Alfred Hawthorne Hill)
British comedian.

Hulk Hogan (Terry Gene Bollea)
Professional wrestler and actor.

William Holden (William Beedle)
Actor. Played in *The Wild Bunch*.

Judy Holliday (Judith Tuvim)
Actress. Played in *Born Yesterday* and *Adam's Rib*.

Hopalong Cassidy (William Lawrence Boyd)
Actor in cowboy movies.

Bob Hope (Leslie Townes Hope)
Actor and comedian.

Harry Houdini (Ehrich Weiss)
Magician.

Rock Hudson (Roy Scherer Jr.)
Actor. The first major American celebrity to admit to having AIDS.

Ehrich Weiss's interest in magic led him to read the book *The Memoirs of Robert-Houdin*, the autobiography of one of the greatest magicians of the day. Weiss discovered that by adding the letter "i" to Houdin, the name in French meant "like." He then changed his name to Houdini, hoping he could be like his mentor.

David Jason (David White)

British actor awarded the title of "Best Actor and Top Television Comedy Actor" in Britain.

Don Johnson (Donnie Wayne Johnson)

Actor, producer, director, and composer. Played in *Miami Vice* and *Nash Bridges*.

Angelina Jolie (Anglenia Jolie Voight)

Actress. Daughter of John Voight. Played Lara Croft in *Tomb Raider*.

Al Jolson (Asa Yoelson)

Actor and singer.

Grace Jones (Grace Mendoza)

Actress. Bond girl in *A View To a Kill*.

James Earl Jones (Todd Jones)

Actor and voice talent. Well known for his beautiful, deep voice. He was the voice of Darth Vader in *Star Wars* and Mufasa in *The Lion King*. He has played in many movies, including *Field of Dreams*.

Spike Jonze (Adam Spiegel)

Director of *Being John Malkovich*, appeared in the movie *Three Kings*, and directed numerous cutting-edge music videos including The Beastie Boys' "Sabotage."

Madeline Kahn (Madeline Gail Wolfson)

Actress and comedian. Appeared in such comedy classics as *Blazing Saddles*.

Boris Karloff (William Pratt)

Actor best known for his creepy appearance in many horror films.

On a scary Halloween night, you might watch a movie starring **William Pratt**, a.k.a. Boris Karloff.

Casey Kasem (Kemal Amin Kasem)

Radio personality. Voice of Shaggy in *Scooby-Doo* cartoons.

Danny Kaye (David Daniel Kaminski)

Actor. Played in *The Court Jester* and *White Christmas*.

Buster Keaton (Joseph Francis Keaton)

Silent film comic actor and film maker.

Diane Keaton (Diane Hall)

Actress and director. Played in *Annie Hall* and *The Godfather*.

Michael Keaton (Michael Douglas)

Actor. Played in *Batman*, *Batman Returns*, and *Mr. Mom*.

Larry King (Larry Zieger)

TV personality.

Ben Kingsley (Krishna Banji)

British actor. Played *Gandhi* in the 1982 movie and starred in *Schindler's List*, as well as many other movies.

Ted Knight (Tadeus Wladyslaw Konopka)

Actor best known for role as Ted Baxter on *The Mary Tyler Moore Show*. Also played in *Caddyshack*.

Veronica Lake (Constance Ockleman)

Actress and producer. Played in *This Gun For Hire* and *Blue Dahlia*.

Dorothy Lamour (Mary Leta Dorothy Slaton)

Actress. Appeared in several movies with Bing Crosby and Bob Hope.

Michael Landon (Eugene Maurice Orowitz)

Best known for his role as Little Joe in *Bonanza* and Pa in *Little House on the Prairie*.

Nathan Lane (Joseph Lane)

Actor, singer, and comedian. Played in *The Bird Cage* with Robin Williams.

Larry (Louis Fienberg)

One of the Three Stooges.

Stan Laurel (Arthur Stanley Jefferson)

A contemporary (and understudy) of Charlie Chaplin. Actor and producer. Part of comedy duo Laurel and Hardy.

Piper Laurie (Rosetta Jacobs)

Actress. Played in *The Hustler*.

Lucy Lawless (Lucille Frances Ryan)

Actress. Played in *Xena: Princess Warrior*.

Bruce Lee (Lee Jun-fan)

Actor famous for his martial arts movies.

> Those interested in martial arts consider **Lee Jun-fan** to be the greatest actor in the field. Jun-fan goes by the pseudonym of Bruce Lee.

Spike Lee (Shelton Jackson Lee)

Director and actor. Directed *Malcolm X*, *Mo' Better Blues*, and *Jungle Fever*.

Janet Leigh (Jeanette Helen Morrison)

Actress. Starred in Hitchcock horror *Psycho*. Married to Tony Curtis, mother to Jamie Lee Curtis.

Jennifer Jason Leigh (Jennifer Lee Morrow)

Actress. Played in *Fast Times At Ridgemont High* and *Single White Female*.

Vivien Leigh (Vivien Mary Hartley)

Actress best known for her role as Scarlett O'Hara in *Gone With The Wind*.

Téa Leoni (Elizabeth Téa Pantleoni)

Actress. Played in *Jurassic Park II* and *Deep Impact*, and on the TV series *The Naked Truth*.

Jerry Lewis (Joseph Levitch)

Actor and comedian. Original lead in *The Nutty Professor*.

Jet Li (Li Lian Jie)

Action movie and martial arts star.

Sophia Loren (Sofia Scicolone)

Oscar-winning actress. Played in *Two Women*, *El Cid*, *Man of La Mancha*, and many other movies.

Peter Lorre (László Löwenstein)

Actor. Played in *Maltese Falcon* and *Casablanca*.

Bela Lugosi (Be'la Ferenc Dezso Blasko)

Horror movie star in classics such as *Dracula*.

Shirley MacLaine (Shirley MacLean Beaty)

Actress. Played in *Terms of Endearment, Postcards from the Edge,* and many other movies. Sister of Warren Beatty, who added an extra "t" to his last name.

Elle MacPherson (Eleanor Gow)

Model and actress.

Lee Majors (Harvey Lee Yeary II)

Actor. Played the title role in *The Six Million Dollar Man* and *Fall Guy.*

Karl Malden (Malden Sekulovich)

Actor. Played in *A Street Car Named Desire.*

Jayne Mansfield (Vera Jane Palmer)

Actress. Played in *The Girl Can't Help It.*

Dean Martin (Dino Crocetti)

Actor. Member of the Rat Pack, with Frank Sinatra, Sammy Davis Jr. and others.

He first appeared in performances under his real name of **Dino Crocetti**. His name underwent an evolution to Dino Martini, and in 1940 to the famous name of Dean Martin.

Tony Martin (Alvin Morris)

Actor and singer. Appeared in film musicals of the 1950s and 60s.

Groucho Marx (Julius Henry Marx)

Comedian: one of the Marx Brothers.

Harpo Marx (Adolph Marx)

Comedian: one of the Marx Brothers.

Zeppo Marx (Herbert Marx)

Yet another Marx brother, Zeppo was the fourth brother in the family. After Gummo dropped out of the act to enter World War I in October of 1918, the brothers recruited Herbert to replace him.

Walter Matthau (Walter Matuschanskayasky)

Actor. Played in *The Odd Couple* (movie version) and *Grumpy Old Men*.

Brini Maxwell (Ben Sander)

TV host and style consultant.

Guy Mitchell (Albert Cernick)

All-around talent of the 1950s and 1960s. Sang solo with several bands and acted in movies.

Moe (Moses Horwitz)

One of the Three Stooges.

Marilyn Monroe (Norma Jeane Mortenson)

When **Norma Jeane** told her mother that she was considering "Marilyn" for a stage name, her mother suggested that it would be complemented by her mother's maiden name, Monroe. So she went with it.

Actress, sex symbol, and pop icon. She starred in many movies and made many appearances. She was married to Joe DiMaggio and Arthur Miller, and supposedly had an affair with President John F. Kennedy.

Demi Moore (Demetria Gene Guynes)

Actress. Got her start on ABC's *General Hospital*. She went on to star in movies such as *Ghost* and *Striptease*. She was married to Bruce Willis, with whom she has three daughters.

> Besides flying saucers, Roswell, New Mexico, has another claim to fame. It is the birthplace of **Demetria Gene Guynes**, better known as Demi Moore.

Rita Moreno (Rosita Dolores Alverio)

Actress. Played in *West Side Story*, and later played on PBS's *The Electric Company*.

Zero Mostel (Samuel Mostel)

Actor. Blacklisted in the 1950s due to his political beliefs.

Mr. T (Lawrence Tero)

Actor. Played in *Rocky III* and *The A-Team*.

Julie Newmar (Julia Charlene Newmeyer)

Actress. Played in *Seven Brides For Seven Brothers*.

Chuck Norris (Carlos Ray)

Actor known for his action flicks.

Elaine Paige (Elaine Bikerstaff)

Actress. Played many of the female leads in musicals by Andrew Lloyd Webber.

Pee-wee Herman (Paul Rubenfeld)

Children's TV host and comedian. A.k.a. Paul Reubens.

Lou Diamond Phillips (Lou Upchurch)

Actor. Played in *Young Guns* and *Young Guns II*.

Mary Pickford (Gladys Smith)
Actress. Married to Douglas Fairbanks.

Roman Polanski (Raimund Liebling)
Director. Directed *Rosemary's Baby*.

Natalie Portman (Natalie Hershlag)
Actress. Played in *Star Wars Episode I: The Phantom Menace, Star Wars Episode II: Attack of The Clones, Star Wars Episode III: Revenge of The Sith*.

Stefanie Powers (Stefdnia Zofija Federkiewicz)
Actress. Played in the TV series *Hart to Hart*.

Tony Randall (Leonard Rosenberg)
Actor. Starred in *The Odd Couple*.

Della Reese (Delloreese Patricia Early)
Actress and singer. Played Tess in *Touched by an Angel*.

> **Della Reese** didn't have a hard time choosing her pseudonym. She took her first name of Delloreese, changed one letter, and divided one name into two.

Vic Reeves (Jim Moir)
British comedian for the BBC.

Debbie Reynolds (Mary Frances Reynolds)
Actress. Played in *Singin' in the Rain* and *The Unsinkable Molly Brown*.

Joan Rivers (Joan Alexandra Molinsky)
TV personality. Coined the phrase "Can we talk?"

Edward G. Robinson (Emanuel Goldenberg)
Actor. Played in *Key Largo* and *Double Indemnity*.

The Rock (Dwayne Douglas Johnson)
Professional wrestler and actor.

Ginger Rogers (Virginia Katherine McMath)
Actress and dancer. Made ten musicals with Fred Astaire.

Roy Rogers (Leonard Slye)
Actor. Made westerns with his wife Dale Evans and his horse Trigger.

Mickey Rooney (Joe Yule Jr.)
Actor. Played in *National Velvet* and *The Adventures of Huck Finn*.

Meg Ryan (Margaret Mary Emily Anne Hyra)
Actress. Best known for role in *When Harry Met Sally*.

> Savage Garden's composer had a crush on **Meg Ryan**, which inspired him to write their song "All Around Me."

Winona Ryder (Winona Laura Horowitz)
Actress. Played in many movies, including *Beetlejuice*, *Mermaids*, and *Reality Bites*.

> **Winona Ryder** was named for her hometown of Winona, Minnesota.

Susan Sarandon (Susan Abigail Tomalin)
Actress. Played in *Thelma and Louise*, *Bull Durham*, and many other movies.

Dick Sargent (Richard Cox)
Actor. Played the second Darrin Stephens on *Bewitched*.

Peter Sellers (Richard Henry Sellers)
Actor. Played in the Pink Panther movies and *Dr. Strangelove*.

Jane Seymour (Joyce Penelope Wilhelmina Frankenburg)

> **Joyce Penelope Wilhelmina Frankenburg** took the name of an English queen for her pseudonym of Jane Seymour.

Actress. Played in *Somewhere in Time* with Christopher Reeve, and starred on the TV series *Dr. Quinn, Medicine Woman*.

Omar Sharif (Michael Shalhoub)

Actor. A.k.a. Omar El-Shariff. Played in *Dr. Zhivago*.

Charlie Sheen (Carlos Irwin Estevez)

Actor, son of Martin Sheen, and brother of Emilio Estevez. Appeared in *Platoon*, *Wall Street*, and *Spin City*.

Martin Sheen (Ramon Estevez)

Actor. Starred in many movies, including *Apocalypse Now*. He also stars in the TV series *West Wing*.

> **Ramon Estevez** (Martin Sheen) took the stage name of Sheen in honor of theologian Bishop Sheen. His son Charlie continued to use the Sheen name, while his brother, Emilio chose to keep his real name of Estevez.

Phil Silvers (Philip Silversmith)

Actor. Played in the TV series *Sgt. Bilko*.

Christian Slater (Christian Michael Leonard Hawkins)

Actor. Star of many box-office hits.

Slim Pickens (Louis Bert Lindley Jr.)

Actor and cowboy. Starred in *Blazing Saddles* and dozens of other films.

Anna Nicole Smith (Vickie Lynn Hogan)
Actress, model, and sensationalist.

Soupy Sales (Milton Supman)
A comedian and actor best known for his daily noontime children's television show, *Lunch With Soupy Sales*. His routines almost always resulted in Soupy receiving a pie in the face.

Kevin Spacey (Kevin Spacey Fowler)
Actor. Played in *Usual Suspects* and *LA Confidential*.

Jill St. John (Jill Oppenheim)
Actress. Bond girl in *Diamonds Are Forever*.

Sylvester Stallone (Michael Sylvester Enzio Stallone)
Actor. Starred in *Rocky* and *Rambo* movies.

Connie Stevens (Concetta Rosalie Ingolia)
Actress. Played in *Rock-A-Bye-Baby*.

Concetta Rosalie Ingolia took the stage name of her father Peter Stevens and became Connie Stevens.

Gale Storm (Josephine Owaissa Cottle)
Actress. Played in *My Little Margie* and *GI Honeymoon*.

Meryl Streep (Mary Louise Streep)
Actress. Played in *Sophie's Choice*, *Silkwood*, and *Bridges of Madison County*.

Robert Taylor (Spangler Arlington Brugh)
Actor. Played in *Camille*.

Rip Torn (Elmore Rual Torn Jr.)

Actor. Played in *Men In Black* and HBO's *The Larry Sanders Show*.

Sophie Tucker (Sophia Kalish)

Vaudeville entertainer.

Lana Turner (Julia Jean Mildred Frances Turner)

Actress. Played in the 1957 movie *Peyton Place*.

Twiggy (Leslie Hornby)

Model. A.k.a. Twiggy Lawson. Nicknamed for her thin figure.

Rudolph Valentino (Rodolpho Gugliemi di Valentina d'Antonguolla)

Actor. Famous movie star of the 1920s.

Jean Claude van Damme (Jean-Claude Camille Francois Van Vavenberg)

Action movie star.

Mamie Van Doren (Joan Lucille Olander)

Actress. Sex symbol and star of several cult films of the 1950s.

Lindsay Wagner (Lindsay Jean Ball)

Actress who starred on the TV series *The Bionic Woman*.

Christopher Walken (Ronald Walken)

Actor and comedian. Played in *The Dead Zone* and *Catch Me If You Can*.

Burt Ward (Hebert John Grevis Jr.)

Played Robin in 1960s TV version of *Batman*.

John Wayne (Marion Robert Morrison)

Actor known for his cowboy roles. Also called "The Duke."

Sigourney Weaver (Susan Weaver)

Actress. Played in the *Alien* movies and *Ghostbusters*.

Raquel Welch (Jo-Raquel Tejada)

Actress, model, and sex symbol. Got her start as a weather forecaster, and went on to play in many movies.

Adam West (William West Anderson)

Played Batman in 1960s TV version of *Batman*.

Vanna White (Vanna Marie Rosich)

TV personality on *Wheel of Fortune*.

Gene Wilder (Jerome Silberman)

Actor and comedian. Made several buddy comedies with Richard Pryor. Was married to Gilda Radner.

Flip Wilson (Clerow Wilson)

Actor and comedian.

Shelley Winters (Shirley Schrift)

Actress. A.k.a. Shelly Winter. Played in *Diary of Anne Frank* and *The Poseidon Adventure*.

Ernie Wise (Ernest Wiseman)

Comedian. Part of the British comedy duo Morecambe and Wise.

Wolfman Jack (Robert Smith)

Hugely popular disc jockey in the 50s and 60s, The Wolfman became a pop icon. He punctuated his broadcasts with howls. This style was modeled, at least in part, on blues man Howlin' Wolf.

Although **Wolfman Jack** was Caucasian, many listeners assumed he was African American, and he chose to keep his real identity a mystery. In 1973 he appeared in *American Graffiti*, allowing the public to see him in a pivotal scene where a main character catches a glimpse of The Wolfman.

Natalie Wood (Natasha Gurdin)

Actress. Played in *Rebel Without a Cause*.

ARTISTS, SCULPTORS, & ARCHITECTS

ARTISTS, SCULPTORS, & ARCHITECTS

ALIAS (REAL NAME)

Aleijandinho (Antonio Francisco Lisboa)
Brazilian sculptor.

Brassai (Gyula Halesz)
Parisian photographer.

Canaletto (Bernado Canale, Giovanni Antonio Canal, and Bernado Belotto)
Venetian artists. The three were father, son, and nephew.

Le Corbusier (Charles Edouard Jeanneret)
Architect, famous for what is now called the International style.

El Greco (Domenikos Theotocopoulos)
Cretan-born painter and sculptor. "El Greco" is Spanish for "the Greek."

Salvador Dali (Salvador Domenec Felip Jacint Dali Domenech)
Surrealist painter.

Erte (Romain de Tirtoff)
Art Deco painter and designer, best known for his set designs in Europe and Hollywood.

Michael Ffolkes (Brian Davis)
Illustrator and cartoonist.

Nuam Gabo (Nuam Neemia Pevsner)
Russian Constructivist. He worked mainly in plastic and created cubist, abstract sculptures.

Giambologna (Jean Boulogne)
A sculptor who is best known for his works with bronze and marble.

Arshile Gorki (Vosanig Manoog Adoian)
Armenian painter.

Juan Gris (Jose Victoriano Gonzales)
Cubist painter.

Jack Higgins (Harry Patterson)
Editorial cartoonist for the *Chicago Sun-Times*.

Emil Nolde (Emil Hansen)
German Expressionist painter.

Mark Rothko (Marcus Rothkovitch)
Contemporary artist, mainly of abstract expressionism.

Il Sodoma (Giovanni Antonio Bazzi)
Italian painter.

Andy Warhol (Andrew Warhola)

American painter and major figure in the pop art movement.

Andy Warhol has certainly had more than his 15 minutes of fame, but is often misquoted. His quote was: "In the future everyone will be world-famous for 15 minutes." He also said "Don't pay attention to what they write about you. Just measure it in inches."

ATHLETES

ATHLETES

ALIAS (REAL NAME)

Kareem Abdul-Jabbar (Ferdinand Lewis "Lew" Alcindor)

7'2" basketball player for the L.A. Lakers. He was famous for his jump hook. He set NBA all-time records for games played, points made, and field goals made.

Muhammed Ali (Cassius Marcellus Clay)

Became the Heavyweight Champion of the world in 1964, when he defeated Sonny Liston.

In 1964, **Cassius Marcellus Clay Jr**. joined the Nation of Islam, and changed his name to Muhammad Ali. In 1966, he refused to serve in the American army in the Vietnam War. He was stripped of his championship belt and his license to box, and sentenced to five years in prison (which was overturned on appeal three years later). In 1970, he was granted a license to box again, following a Supreme Court victory wherein he was granted the right to refuse military service.

Babe Ruth (George Harman Ruth)

American baseball player. He was one of the first five players elected to the Baseball Hall of Fame and he was the first player to hit over 50 home runs in one season.

Yogi Berra (Lawrence Peter Berra)

Baseball player and manager of the New York Yankees.

> Cartoon character **Yogi Bear** is named after the Hall of Fame manager and player Yogi Berra.

Big Daddy (Shirley Crabtree)

Professional wrestler.

Catweazle (Gary Cooper)

Professional wrestler.

Jack Dempsey (William Harrison Dempsey)

Became the Heavyweight Champion of the world on July 4, 1919 when he defeated Jess Willard.

Kid Gavilan (Gerardo Gonzalez)

Cuban boxer and world Welterweight Champion.

Joe Louis (Joseph Louis Barrow)

Heavyweight Champion of the world from 1937 to 1949. Nicknamed The Brown Bomber.

Dame Alicia Markova (Lilian Alicia Marks)

Russian ballet dancer who was for years considered the greatest classical ballerina of the Western world.

Kendo Nagasaki (Peter Thornley)

Professional wrestler.

Pele (Edson Arantes do Nascimento)

Brazilian soccer player considered by some to be the king of the sport.

Rocky Graziano (Thomas Rocco Barbella)

American Middleweight championship boxer.

Rocky Marciano (Rocco Marchegiano)

Became the Heavyweight Champion of the world on September 23, 1952, when he defeated Jersey Joe Walcott.

Sugar Ray Leonard (Ray Charles Leonard)

American boxing champion. Born Ray Charles Leonard, after the singing legend Ray Charles. Leonard later adopted the nickname used by Sugar Ray Robinson.

Sugar Ray Robinson (Walker Smith Jr.)

An American boxer who is the holder of many boxing records, including the one for the most times being a champion in a division, winning the world Middleweight division title 5 times. He also won the world Welterweight title once.

Daley Thompson (Francis Morgan Thompson)

Former British decathlete. He won consecutive gold medals at the 1980 and 1984 Olympic Games, and broke the world record for the event four times.

Jersey Joe Walcott (Arnold Raymond Cream)

Became the Heavyweight Champion of the world on July 18, 1951, when he defeated Ezzard Charles.

SINGERS, MUSICIANS, & COMPOSERS

SINGERS, MUSICIANS, & COMPOSERS

8 Ball (Premro Smith)

Rapper.

50 Cent (Curtis Jackson)

Rap and hip-hop artist. First artist signed to Eminem's label Shady Records.

50 Cent (pronounced "fiddy cent") gets his name from gangster 50 Cent of Fort Green Projects in Brooklyn, New York.

Tori Amos (Myra Ellen Amos)

Singer, pianist, and songwriter.

Andre 3000 (Benjamin Andre)

Part of the rap duo OutKast from Atlanta, Georgia.

Adam Ant (Stuart Leslie Goddard)

Lead singer for Adam and the Ants. Had hit with "Goody Two Shoes."

Adam Ant got his stage name from the British television series *Adam Adamant Lives!*

Little Anthony (Jerome Anthony Gourdine)
R&B singer. Sang "Tears On My Pillow" and "Shimmy Shimmy Ko-Ko Bop."

Fiona Apple (Fiona Apple Maggart)
Singer.

Tina Arena (Filipina Lydia Arena)
Pop singer.

Kon Artis (Denaun Porter)
Hip-hop artist.

Eric B (Eric Barrier)
Rap and hip-hop artist.

Babyface (Kenneth Brian Edmonds)
Singer, songwriter, and producer.

Erykah Badu (Erica Wright)
Actress and music producer. Appeared in several films as herself.

LaVern Baker (Delores Williams)
Second woman inducted into Rock and Roll Hall of Fame.

Afrika Bambaataa (Kevin Donovan)
Rapper, DJ, and music producer. He was instrumental in the early development of rap music.

Toni Basil (Antonia Basilotta)
Choreographer, singer, and one hit-wonder with song "Mickey."

Lance Bass (James Lansten Bass)
Member of pop boy band *NSYNC.

Beck (Beck David Campbell Hansen)
Singer and guitarist.

Pat Benatar (Patricia Andrejewski)
Rock singer and guitarist.

Tony Bennett (Anthony Dominick Benedetto)
Classic vocalist in America since the 1950s. Released such hits as "I Left My Heart in San Francisco."

Tony Bennett is not only a singer, but also a painter. He signs his paintings with his real last name, Benedetto, and when he sings he uses his stage name, Bennett, which means "Blessed."

Brooke Benton (Benjamin Franklin Peay)
Jazz and pop singer.

Chuck Berry (Charles Edward Berry)
Guitarist, singer, and composer. One of the most influential rockers in the U.S.

Jello Biafra (Eric Boucher)
Lead singer for the Dead Kennedys and a solo artist.

Big Boi (Antwan Patton)
Part of the rap duo OutKast from Atlanta, Georgia.

The Big Bopper (Jiles Perry Richardson)

Singer and DJ. Sang "Chantilly Lace." Died in a plane crash with Buddy Holly and Ritchie Valens.

The Big Bopper took his name as a gimmick because he noticed all the college kids doing a dance they called "the Bop."

Bizzy Bone (Byron McCane)

Hip-hop artist, formerly with group Bone Thugs-n-Harmony.

Cilla Black (Priscilla White)

Singer.

Frank Black (Charles Michael Kitridge Thompson IV)

Former leader of The Pixies. Also known as Black Francis.

Blackberry (Berlenda Nikki Gadson)

R&B and soul artist.

Blondie (Debbie Harry)

Lead singer of the band Blondie.

Kurtis Blow (Curtis Walker)

Rap artist. One of the first rap stars.

Michael Bolton (Michael Bolotin)

Singer.

Jon Bon Jovi (John Bongiovi)

Rock/pop star and actor.

Sonny Bono (Salvatore Phillip Bono)

Singer, actor, and later politician. Ex-husband of Cher.

Early in their careers, **Sonny** and **Cher Bono** were known as Cleo and Caesar.

Bono (Paul Hewson)

Lead singer of band U2.

Pat Boone (Charles Eugene Boone)

Singer and pop star.

Victor Borge (Borge Rosenbaum)

Comedian and pianist.

David Jones, a.k.a. David Bowie, wanted a name different than Davy Jones of the Monkees, so he chose Bowie after the legendary Jim Bowie.

Bow Wow (Shad Gregory Moss)

Rap artist. Also called Lil Bow Wow.

David Bowie (David Jones)

Rock artist and actor.

Boxcar Willie (Lecil Travis Martin)

Country-western artist.

Boxcar Willie considered his songs "hobo" music, as if seeing the world go by on a freight train.

Boy George (George Alan O'Dowd)

Pop star, formerly of Culture Club.

Billy Bragg (Steven William Bragg)

British punk rock star and folk singer.

Brandy (Brandy Rayana Norwood)
R&B and soul artist.

B-Real (Louis Freese)
Rap artist in group Cypress Hill.

Teresa Brewer (Teresa Breuer)
Singer. Best known for best-selling hit "Till I Waltz Again With You."

Foxy Brown (Inga Marchaud)
Rap and hip-hop artist.

Buckwheat Zydeco (Stanley Joseph Dural Jr.)
Singer.

Burning Spear (Winston Rodney)
Singer and musician. Jamaican roots rock and reggae.

Busta Rhymes (Trevor Tahiem Smith Jr.)
Rap artist.

Canibus (Germaine Williams)
Rap artist.

Captain Beefheart (Don Van Vliet)
Singer. Known for his mixture of beat poetry, jazz, and R&B.

Ray Charles (Ray Charles Robinson)
Famous gospel, soul, and R&B singer and pianist.

Ray Charles shortened his name so he wouldn't be confused with the famous boxer Sugar Ray Robinson.

Cher (Cherilyn Sarkisian LaPier)

Pop superstar and actress. Part of television duo "Sonny and Cher."

Neneh Cherry (Neneh Mariann Karlsson)

Rap artist. R&B singer.

Chilli (Rozonda Ocielian Thomas)

R&B artist in the group TLC.

Chingy (Howard Bailey Jr.)

Rap artist.

Chubby Checker (Ernest Evans)

Sang "The Twist."

Chuck D (Carlton Ridenhour)

Rap artist in group Public Enemy and political activist.

Eric Clapton (Eric Patrick Clapp)

Influential guitarist and singer.

Jimmy Cliff (James Chambers)

Jamaican reggae musician.

Patsy Cline (Virginia Patterson Hensley)

Classic country singer. Sang "Crazy" and "I Fall To Pieces."

Nat King Cole (Nathaniel Adams Coles)

Sang the holiday standard "The Christmas Song."

Bootsy Collins (William Collins)

Member of Rock and Roll Hall of Fame. Funk bassist, singer, and songwriter.

Colonel Tom Parker (Andreas Cornelius van Kujik)

Manager of Elvis Presley.

Colonel Tom Parker's job before managing Elvis included working for the circus, catching dogs, and owning a pet cemetery.

Shawn Colvin (Shanna Colvin)

Singer, songwriter, and guitarist.

Perry Como (Perino Roland Como)

Singer.

Coolio (Artis Ivey Jr.)

Rap artist.

Alice Cooper (Vincent Damon Furnier)

Singer and shock-rocker.

Perhaps Vincent Damon Furnier chose the name **Alice Cooper** because it conjures up images of a sweet-looking girl hiding a hatchet behind her back!

Elvis Costello (Declan Patrick Aloysius McManus)

Musician, singer, and songwriter.

Elvis Costello got his pseudonym by combining the first name of Elvis Presley and his mother's maiden name of Costello.

Count Basie (William Basie)

A leading figure of the swing era in jazz and, alongside Duke Ellington, a representative of big band style.

David Crosby (David Van Cortland)

Singer, formerly in Crosby, Stills, and Nash.

Christopher Cross (Christopher Geppert)
Singer. Sang "Sailing" and "Theme from Author."

Stan Cullimore (Ian Cullimore)
Original member of The Housemartins.

Daddy G (Grant Marshall)
Blues guitarist.

Taylor Dane (Lesley Wonderman)
Singer.

Bobby Darin (Walden Robert Cassotto)
Rock star of the "golden age of rock" in the 1950s and 1960s.

Miles Davis (Dewey Davis III)
Trumpeter.

Bobby Day (Robert Byrd)
Doo-wop star best known for his hit "Rockin' Robin."

Joey Dee (Joseph DiNicola)
Member of The Starlighters.

Kiki Dee (Pauline Matthews)
Singer best known for hit "Don't Go Breaking My Heart," performed with Elton John.

John Denver (Henry John Deutschendorf Jr.)
Folk singer.

John Denver looked for a name to record under, including John Sommerville, before he decided to take his name for the Rocky Mountain capital of Colorado.

Bo Diddley (Otha Ellas Bates McDaniel)

Pop and blues musician. Sang "Who Do You Love?"

> It is rumored that **Bo Diddley** took his name from a one-stringed African guitar. He managed to work his name into several of his song and album titles, as well as some of his lyrics.

Dido (Dido Florian Cloud de Bounevialle Armstrong)

Singer and songwriter, best known for hit "Thank You."

Ani DiFranco (Angela Marie DiFranco)

Singer and songwriter.

Disco Tex (Joseph Moses Montarez Jnr)

Lead singer for the oldies band Disco Tex and the Sex-O-Lettes, who sang "I Wanna Dance Wit' Choo."

DJ Headliner (Timothy Barnwell)

Afrocentric Rap artist in the group Arrested Development.

DJ Shadow (Josh Davis)

DJ and hip-hop personality.

DJ Yella (Antoine Carraby)

Drummer, producer, and part of group N.W.A.

DMC (Darryl McDaniel)

Rap artist in group Run DMC.

DMX (Earl Simmons)

Better known as a rapper, but also an actor and producer. Starred in *Romeo Must Die*.

Sen Dog (Sennen Reyes)
Rap artist in group Cypress Hill.

Nate Dogg (Nathaniel Dawayne Hale)
Rap artist.

Thomas Dolby (Thomas Morgan Robertson)
Singer, best known for his hit "She Blinded Me With Science."

Donovan (Donovan Leitch)
British folk singer best known for "Mellow Yellow."

Dr. Dre (Andre Young)
Hip-hop artist and producer. Former member of N.W.A.

Bob Dylan (Robert Zimmerman)
Rock artist and folk singer.

Sheena Easton (Sheena Shirley Orr)
Actress and pop singer. Hit single "Morning Train."

Eazy-E (Eric Wright)
Rap artist in the group N.W.A.

The Edge (David Howell Evans)
Guitarist of U2.

Eek-A-Mouse (Ripton Joseph Hilton)
Jamaican reggae-rapper and singer.

Duke Ellington (Edward Kennedy Ellington)
Musician.

Missy Elliott (Melissa Elliott)

Rap artist.

Eminem (Marshall Mathers III)

Hip-hop artist. Starred in the semi-autobiographical movie *8 Mile*.

Eminem's real name is Marshall Mathers. He used his initials to come up with his original stage name of M&M, but later changed the spelling to Eminem.

Enya (Eithne ní Bhraonáin)

New age performer.

David Essex (David Alvbert Cook)

Singer and recording artist.

Gloria Estefan (Gloria Fajardo)

Singer, The Miami Sound Machine.

Little Eva (Eve Narcissus Boyd)

Put out the hit single "The Loco-Motion" in 1962.

Eve (Eve Jihan Jeffers)

Lyricist, rapper, and actress.

Everlast (Eric Schrody)

Former member of rap group House of Pain. Now known for his blend of rock, rap, and blues.

Falco (Johann Holzel)

Singer, best known for his hit "Rock Me Amadeus."

Falco took his name from an East German ski jumper.

Perry Farrell (Perry Bernstein)

Lead singer of Jane's Addiction and founder of traveling music festival Lollapalooza.

Fatboy Slim (Quentin Cook, later Norman Cook)

DJ, dance, and techno artist.

Fats Domino (Antoine Domino)

Singer.

Fats Waller (Thomas Wright Waller)

Jazz pianist in the 1930s.

Richard Fearless (Richard Maguire)

Hip-hop artist.

Freddie Fender (Baldemar G. Huerta)

Country-western artist.

Johnny Fingers (John Moylett)

Irish keyboard player who attracted attention because he wore pajamas onstage during his concerts with The Boomtown Rats.

Fish (Derek William Dick)

Singer.

Flavor Flav (William Drayton)

Hip-hop artist. Member of Public Enemy.

Flea (Michael Balzary)

Bassist for rock band Red Hot Chili Peppers.

Flesh-n-Bone (Stanley Howse)

Hip-hop artist with group Bone Thugs-n-Harmony.

Samantha Fox (Stacia Micula)

Singer.

Connie Francis (Concetta Franconero)

One of the best selling female artists of all time. Sang "Who's Sorry Now?"

Doug E. Fresh (Douglas E. Davis)

Rap artist.

Kenny G (Kenny Gorelick)

Saxophonist.

Leif Garrett (Leif Per Narvik)

Pop star and teen idol in the 1980s.

Marvin Gaye (Marvin Pentz Gay Jr.)

R&B artist.

Crystal Gayle (Brenda Gail Webb)

Country-western artist. Sister of Loretta Lynn.

Gloria Gaynor (Gloria Fowles)

Pop singer. Best known for her hit "I Will Survive."

Bobbie Gentry (Roberta Streeter)

Classic country music star of the 20th century. Sang "Ode To Billy Joe."

Stan Getz (Stanley Gayetzsky)
Pianist.

Barry Gibb (Douglas Gibb)
Member of The Bee Gees.

Dizzy Gillespie (John Birks Gillespie)
Trumpeter.

Lesley Gore (Lesley Goldstein)
Singer best known for "It's My Party."

Eydie Gorme (Edith Gormezano)
Singer.

Bill Graham (Wolfgang Wolodja Grajonka)
Night-club founder and music promoter.

Dobie Gray (Leonard Victor Ainsworth)
Singer best known for hit "Drift Away."

Macy Gray (Natalie Renee McIntyre)
Singer.

Woody Guthrie (Woodrow Wilson Guthrie)
Entertained during the Great Depression. Known for his guitar work and his controversial social commentary and wry humor.

Buddy Guy (George Guy)
Blues guitarist.

Daryl Hall (Daryl Franklin Hohl)
Guitarist with Hall & Oates.

Richard Hell (Richard Meyers)
Rock singer and producer.

Billie Holiday (Eleanora Fagan Holiday)
Popular jazz singer in the 1950s.

Buddy Holly (Charles Hardin Holly)
Singer. Died in a plane crash at the height of his career.

Nellee Hooper (Paul Andrew Hooper)
DJ and producer.

Howlin' Wolf (Chester Burnett)
Blues singer.

Engelbert Humperdinck (Gerry Dorsey)
Singer.

Engelbert Humperdinck took his name for the German composer of the same name, best known for the opera Hansel and Gretel.

Janis Ian (Janis Eddy Fink)
Folk rocker. Had hit with "At Seventeen."

Ice Cube (O'Shea Jackson)
Rap artist and actor.

Not to be confused...
Ice Cube is a former member of N.W.A. and has appeared in movies such as Three Kings and Barbershop.
Ice-T once headed the thrash-metal band Bodycount and now stars on the T.V. series Law & Order: SVU.

Ice T (Tracy Marrow)
Rap, hip-hop artist, and actor.

Billy Idol (William Broad)

Rock star known for dark hits such as "White Wedding."

> **Billy Idol** chose his name because of comments on a school report card calling him "idle," but decided on "Idol" instead.

Iggy Pop (James Jewel Osterberg Jr.)

Lead singer of Iggy & The Stooges.

Ja Rule (Jeffrey Atkins)

Rap artist. Most well-known for his hit "Put It On Me."

Jam Master Jay (Jason Mizell)

Actor and composer. Member of Run DMC.

Etta James (Jamesetta Hawkins)

Gospel, blues, and jazz singer.

Rick James (James Ambrose Johnson)

Singer, best known for his hit "Super Freak."

Jay-Z (Shawn Corey Carter)

Rap artist.

Blind Lemon Jefferson (Clarence Jefferson)

Popular blues artist of the 1920s.

Jelly Roll Morton (Ferdinand Joseph Lemott)

Jazz pianist.

Joan Jett (Joan Larkin)

Rock star. With Joan Jett and the Blackhearts, she was famous for such songs as "I Love Rock 'n' Roll."

Jewel (Jewel Kilcher)
Rock and pop artist.

Elton John (Reginald Kenneth Dwight)
Rock and pop superstar.

> Reginald Kenneth Dwight changed his name to **Elton John** as homage to saxophonist Elton Dean and singer Long John Baldry, fellow "bluesologists."

Holly Johnson (William Johnson)
Lead singer of Frankie Goes To Hollywood. Had a hit in the 80s with song "Relax."

Oran "Juice" Jones (Roger Davis)
A disco artist who made it big with his only hit "The Rain."

Tom Jones (Thomas Jones Woodward)
Singer.

Wynonna Judd (Christina Claire Judd)
A.k.a. Wynonna Country. Singer. Along with her mother, formed The Judds. Sister of actress Ashley Judd.

Judge Dread (Alex Hughes)
British reggae artist.

Juvenile (Terius Gray)
Rap artist.

Alicia Keys (Alicia Augello Cook)
Singer.

Chaka Khan (Yvette Marie Stevens)

Singer. Sang "Tell Me Something Good" and I'm Every Woman."

Albert King (Albert Nelson)

Blues guitarist.

Ben E. King (Benjamin Earl Nelson)

Soul and pop singer, originally with the Drifters. Best known for the hit "Stand by Me," which he sang and co-composed.

Carole King (Carole Klein)

Singer.

Freddie King (Frederick Christian)

Blues guitarist.

King Ad-Rock (Adam Horovitz)

Actor and songwriter. Member of the Beastie Boys.

King Curtis (Curtis Ousley)

Saxophonist.

Kinky Friedman (Richard F. Friedman)

Singer, songwriter, and novelist who rose to cult fame as a country western singer. He recently began a campaign for Governor of Texas, with the campaign slogan "How hard can it be?"

Kool Moe Dee (Mohandas Dewese)

Rap artist.

Krayzie Bone (Anthony Henderson)
Hip-hop artist with group Bone Thugs-n-Harmony.

Martha La Velle (Martha Reeves)
Singer.

Patti LaBelle (Patricia Louise Holt)
Disco-pop singer. Best-known for "New Attitude."

Cleo Laine (Clementina Dinah Campbell)
Singer and actress.

Blackie Lawless (Steven Duren)
Singer and guitarist for the band W.A.S.P.

Steve Lawrence (Sidney Leibowitz)
Singer. Married to Edie Gorme.

Layzie Bone (Steven Howse)
Hip-hop artist with group Bone Thugs-n-Harmony.

Leadbelly (Hiddie Ledberrer)
A violent, often erratic man, Leadbelly was "discovered" in prison and twice pardoned on homicide or attempted homicide charges when he sang for the governor of the state holding him. He signed a recording contract and made folk records for many years.

Brenda Lee (Brenda Mae Tarpley)
Classic country artist. Sang holiday classic "Rockin' Around the Christmas Tree."

Peggy Lee (Norma Delores Egstrom)
Singer. Sang "Fever" and "Is That All There Is?"

Tommy Lee (Tommy Lee Bass)
Former drummer of Motley Crue. On-again, off-again husband of Pam Anderson.

Left Eye (Lisa Nicole Lopes)
Singer, member of the original TLC until her death in a car crash.

> The band TLC got its name from each band member's first name: T-Boz, Left-Eye, and Chilli.

Lemmy (Ian Kilminster)
Founding member and leader of heavy-metal group Motorhead.

Huey Lewis (Hugh Anthony Craig III)
Pop star with group Huey Lewis and the News.

Liberace (Wladziu Lee Valentino Liberace)
Pianist.

Lil Kim (Kimberly Denise Jones)
Pop and rap artist.

Little Richard (Richard Wayne Penniman)
Rock and pop artist.

LL Cool J (James Todd Smith)
Pop and rap artist.

> The two Ls in **L.L. Cool J** stand for Ladies Love.

Courtney Love (Love Michelle Harrison)
Singer and guitarist, formerly with the band Hole. Widow of Kurt Cobain.

Lene Lovich (Lili-Marlene Premilovich)

Singer.

Ludacris (Chris Bridges)

Rap artist.

Lulu (Marie Lawrie)

Singer. Sang "To Sir With Love."

Lydia Lunch (Lydia Koch)

Singer.

Annabella Lwin (Myant Myant Aye Dunn-Lwin)

Vocalist for Bow Wow Wow who sang "I Want Candy."

Madonna (Madonna Louise Veronica Ciccone)

Singer, sometimes called the "Queen of Pop."

Madonna has recently adopted the ancient Hebrew name of Esther. Madonna's mother, also named Madonna, died at the age of 30 from cancer. In an interview she said, "I wanted to attach myself to the energy of a different name." Her new name translates as "star."

Magic Sam (Samuel Maghett)

Blues singer.

Magoo (Melvin Barcliff)

Rap and hip-hop artist.

Mama Cass Elliott (Ellen Naomi Cohen)

Singer with The Mamas and the Papas.

Barry Manilow (Barry Alan Pinkus)

Pop singer of such songs as "Mandy" and "Copacabana."

Manfred Mann (Michael Lubowitz)

R&B keyboard player in the band Manfred Mann's Earth Band in the 1960s.

Marilyn Manson (Brian Warner)

Glam rocker, known for his controversial lyrics.

Ziggy Marley (David Marley)

Reggae artist; son of Bob Marley.

Mick Mars (Bob Allen Deal)

Guitarist for Motley Crue.

Marilyn Manson took his name by combining the first name of female pop icon Marilyn Monroe and the last name of serial killer Charles Manson. He did this based on the belief that pop stars and serial killers receive the same notoriety.

Martika (Martha Marrero)

TV star of Kids, Inc. Was a one-hit wonder in the 80s with "Toy Soldiers."

Ricky Martin (Enrique Jose Martin Morales IV)

Pop artist, soap opera star, and heartthrob; once in group Menudo. Became a household name in the U.S. after the success of his song "Livin' La Vida Loca."

Mase (Vincent Lamond Mason)

Rapper. Protégé of P. Diddy.

Master P (Percy Miller Sr.)

Rap artist and producer.

Maxi Priest (Max Elliot)
R&B singer.

Maxim Reality (Keeti Palmer)
Hip-hop artist.

MC Hammer (Stanley Kirk Burrell)
Rap and pop artist. Best known for hit "Can't Touch This."

M.C. Hammer was once a bat boy for the Oakland Athletics.

MC Lyte (Lana Moorer)
Rap and hip-hop artist.

MC Ren (Lorenzo Patterson)
Rap artist in the group N.W.A.

MCA (Adam Yach)
Member of the Beastie Boys.

Roger McGuinn (Jim McGuinn)
Prior to forming the Byrds, toured and performed folk music with the Limeliters, Chad Mitchell Trio, and Bobby Darin as a guitarist and banjo player.

Meat Loaf (Marvin Lee Aday)
Rock singer and actor.

Although there are several rumors about how **Meat Loaf** got his name, the most popular is that his father nicknamed him "Meat" when he was 2, and his school mates turned it into "Meat Loaf."

Melle Mel (Melvin Glover)
Singer.

Memphis Slim (Peter Chatman)

Blues singer and pianist.

Freddie Mercury (Faroukh Bulsara)

Singer, musician, and member of Queen.

> Although Peter Chatman performed under the name **Memphis Slim**, he published his songs under his birth name.

Ethel Merman (Ethel Zimmerman)

Singer.

Method Man (Clifford Smith)

Rap artist. Member of The Wu-Tang Clan.

George Michael (Georgios Kyriacos Panayiotou)

Pop singer. Former member of Wham!

Mike D (Michael Diamond)

In hip-hop/rock group the Beastie Boys.

Buddy Miles (George Miles)

Singer.

Carmen Miranda (Maria de Carmo, Miranda de Cunha)

South American singer.

Joni Mitchell (Roberta Joan Anderson)

Folk singer.

Moby (Richard Melville Hall)

Techno artist.

> **Moby** got his performing name because he is a relative of Herman Melville, author of Moby Dick.

Van Morrison (George Ivan Morrison)
Singer and songwriter.

Mr. Biggs (Ellis William)
Hip-hop artist.

Muggs (Lawrence Muggerud)
Rap and hip-hop artist in the group Cypress Hill.

Mushroom (Andrew Vowles)
Hip-hop artist.

Mystikal (Michael Tyler)
Rap artist.

Nas (Nasir Jones)
Rap artist.

Vince Neil (Vince Neil Wharton)
Singer for the band Motley Crue.

Nelly (Cornell Haynes Jr.)
Rap artist.

Juice Newton (Judy Cohen)
Singer. Sang "Queen of Hearts" and "Angel of the Morning."

Stevie Nicks (Stephanie Lynn Nicks)
Rock singer; former member of Fleetwood Mac.

Notorious B.I.G. (Christopher Wallace)

Rap artist. Also known as Biggie Small. Biggie was rumored to be involved in the murder of Tupac, and he was killed shortly thereafter.

Gary Numan (Gary Anthony James Webb)

Singer. A one-hit wonder in the 80s with "Cars."

Billy Ocean (Leslie Sebastian Charles)

First Caribbean singer to be accepted by MTV, had several hits in the 80s.

Tony Orlando (Michael Anthony Orlando Cassivitis)

Pop singer with Tony Orlando and Dawn. Best known for "Tie a Yellow Ribbon."

Ozzy Osborne (Johnathan Michael Osborne)

Heavy Metal icon since his days with Black Sabbath, now star of hit MTV reality series The Osbornes.

Patti Page (Clara Ann Fowler)

Singer.

Gram Parsons (Cecil Connor)

Country rock musician. Influential in the fusing of rock and country music.

Les Paul (Lester Polfuss)

Guitarist. Creator of the Les Paul electric guitar.

Pepa (Sandra Denton)

R&B singer in the group Salt-N-Pepa.

Edith Piaf (Edith Giovanna Gassion)

Singer.

Pink (Alecia Moore)

Singer.

Buster Poindexter (David Johansen)

Member of The New York Dolls.

Poly Styrene (Marion Elliot)

Singer with UK punk band X-Ray Spex.

Posdnuos (Kelvin Mercer)

Hip-hop artist.

Prince (Prince Rogers Nelson)

Pop and rock singer. Later dropped his name, and was referred to as "the artist formerly known as Prince." Now known as Prince again.

Prince Paul (Paul Houston)

Rap artist.

Professor Griff (Richard Griffin)

Rap and hip-hop artist. Member of Public Enemy.

Puff Daddy (Sean "Puffy" John Combs)

Rap artist and pop icon. Also called P. Diddy.

? (Rudy Balderrama)

Lead singer of ? and the Mysterians. Best known for hit single "96 Tears."

? claims to be a Martian, and says he once lived with the dinosaurs. Somewhat of an eccentric recluse, he is never seen in public without wearing sunglasses.

Q-Tip (Jonathan Davis Kamal IV)

Hip-hop artist, member of A Tribe Called Quest.

Queen Latifah (Dana Owens)

Singer, actress, and Cover Girl model.

Raheim (Guy Todd Williams)

Rap artist.

Rakim (William Griffin)

Rap artist.

Dee Dee Ramone (Douglas Colvin)

Rock artist in group The Ramones.

Joey Ramone (Jeffrey Hyman)

Rock artist in group The Ramones.

Johnny Ramone (John Cummings)

Rock artist in group The Ramones.

The band **The Ramones** took their band name from Paul McCartney, who used to call himself Paul Ramon. The band members all took their last names from the band, although they were not actually brothers.

Marky Ramone (Marc Bell)

Rock artist in group The Ramones.

Ricky Ramone (Richard Beau)

Rock artist in group The Ramones.

Tommy Ramone (Thomas Erdelyi)

Vocals, drummer, and producer for The Ramones.

Shabba Ranks (Rexton Fernando Gordon)
Reggae artist.

Redman (Reggie Noble)
Rap artist.

Lou Reed (Louis Firbank)
Rock star in group the Velvet Underground.

Trent Reznor (Michael Trent Reznor)
Rock artist in group Nine Inch Nails.

Nick Rhodes (Nicholas James Bates)
Member of Duran Duran.

Tex Ritter (Maurice Woodward Ritter)
Classic country-western artist. Father of actor John Ritter.

Smokey Robinson (William Robinson)
Legendary R&B singer.

Kid Rock (Robert James Ritchie)
Rock and rap superstar.

Rockwell (Kennedy Gordy)
Pop star. Son of Motown chief Barry Gordy.

Henry Rollins (Henry Garfield)
Singer.

Axl Rose (William Bruce Rose)
Singer for Guns N' Roses.

Diana Ross (Diane Ernestine Earle)

R&B/pop singer. Former member of The Supremes.

Johnny Rotten (John Lydon)

Iconoclastic lead singer for the Sex Pistols.

> **Johnny Rotten** got his nickname from the state of his teeth.

Kelly Rowland (Kelendria Rowland)

Member of Destiny's Child, appeared in the movie *Freddy vs. Jason.*

Run (Joseph Simmons)

Member of rap group Run-DMC.

Sade (Helen Folasade Adu)

Jazz and R&B singer.

Salt (Cheryl James)

R&B singer in the group Salt-N-Pepa.

Leo Sayer (Gerard Hugh Sayer)

Soul, country, and folk singer.

Screamin' Jay Hawkins (Jalacy Hawkins)

Novelty singer, best known for "I Put a Spell on You."

Seal (Sealhenry Olusegun Olumide Samuel)

Soul and pop artist.

Steve Severin (Steven Bailey)

Member of Sioxsie and the Banshees.

David Seville (Ross Bagdasarian)

Created Alvin and the Chipmunks.

Shaggy (Orville Richard Burrell)

Singer.

Del Shannon (Charles Westover)

Singer. Best known for hit "Runaway."

Artie Shaw (Arthur Jacob Arkshawsky)

Jazz clarinetist, composer, bandleader, and writer.

Shock G (Gregory Jacobs)

Member of rap group Digital Underground.

Michelle Shocked (Karen Michelle Johnson)

Singer and songwriter.

Too Short (Todd Swan)

Rapper.

Gene Simmons (Chaim Witz, later Gene Klein)

Rock star, leader of KISS, and bass player.

Nina Simone (Eunice Kathleen Waymon)

Pianist and singer.

Siouxsie Sioux (Susan Janet Ballion)

Rock artist in Siouxsie and the Banshees.

Sir Mix-A-Lot (Anthony Ray)

Rap artist.

Sisqo (Mark Durell Andrews)
Rap artist.

Nikki Sixx (Frank Carlton Serafino Ferranno)
Bass player for Motley Crue.

Slash (Saul Hudson)
Rock guitarist, formerly with Guns N' Roses.

Grace Slick (Grace Barnett Wing)
Rock artist; singer in Jefferson Airplane.

Snoop Doggy Dogg (Cordazer Calvin Broadus)
Rap artist. A.k.a. Snoop Dogg.

Phoebe Snow (Phoebe Laub)
Singer, guitarist, and songwriter.

Ronnie Spector (Veronica Bennett)
Singer, best known for hit "Be My Little Baby." Ex-wife of Phil Spector.

Speech (Todd Thomas)
Afrocentric Rap artist in the group Arrested Development.

Baby Spice (Emma Lee Bunton)
Member of The Spice Girls.

Ginger Spice (Geraldine Estelle Halliwell)
Member of The Spice Girls.

Posh Spice (Victoria Caroline Adams)

Member of The Spice Girls.

Scary Spice (Melanie Janine Brown)

Member of The Spice Girls.

Sporty Spice (Melanie Jayne Chisholm)

Member of The Spice Girls.

Spindarella (Deidre Roper)

DJ of Salt-N-Pepa.

Dusty Springfield (Mary O'Brien)

Soul artist. Sang "Son Of A Preacher Man."

Dusty Springfield took her name from the musical group she was in called The Springfields.

Edwin Starr (Charles Hatcher)

Soul artist.

Ringo Starr (Richard Starkey)

Member and drummer for the Beatles.

It is believed that **Cat Stevens**, now Yusef Islam, converted to Islam after he was saved from drowning.

Cat Stevens (Steven Demetri Georgiou)

Singer now known as Yusuf Islam. Sang "Peace Train."

Before becoming famous, **Sting** was an English teacher and a grave digger. He once performed wearing a black and yellow jersey, and a fellow band member said he looked like a bee, thus the name Sting.

Sting (Gordon Matthew Sumner)

Rock/pop artist, lead singer for The Police.

Sly Stone (Sylvester Stewart)
Leader of the soul group Sly and The Family Stone.

Izzy Stradlin (Jeff Isabelle)
Former guitarist for Guns N' Roses.

Joe Strummer (John Graham Mellor)
Leader of punk band The Clash.

Donna Summer (LaDonna Andrea Gaines)
Pop/disco star.

Taj Mahal (Henry St. Clair Fredericks)
Blues singer, songwriter, and composer.

T-Boz (Tionne Watkins)
R&B artist in the group TLC.

Terminator X (Norman Lee Rogers)
DJ of Public Enemy.

Tammi Terrell (Thomasina Montgomery)
Best remembered as Marvin Gaye's duet partner on songs including "Ain't No Mountain High Enough" and "Your Precious Love."

Johnny Thunders (John Genzalli)
Singer and front man for first The New York Dolls, then the Heartbreakers.

Tiny Tim (Herbert Buckingham Khaury)
Novelty singer. Sang "Tip Toe Through The Tulips."

Tone-Loc (Anthony Smith)

Rap/pop artist best known for hits "Funky Cold Medina" and "Wild Thing."

Peter Tork (Peter Halston Thorkelson)

Singer with the group The Monkees.

Peter Tosh (Winston Hubert McIntosh)

Jamaican-born singer who has been classified as a Bob Marley with more edge. Advocate of legalized marijuana and human rights.

Randy Travis (Randy Bruce Traywick)

Country-western artist.

Tricky (Adrian Thaws)

Music producer.

Trugoy the Dove (David Jude Jolicoeur)

Songwriter.

Tupac Shakur (Lesane Parish Crooks)

Rap artist.

Ike Turner (Izear Luster Turner)

Pianist, guitarist, bandleader, talent scout, and record producer. Ex-husband of Tina Turner.

Tina Turner (Annie Mae Bullock)

Pop artist.

Shania Twain (Eileen Regina Edwards, later Eileen Regina Twain)

Country-western artist.

Conway Twitty (Harold Jenkins)

Country-western singer.

Conway Twitty took his name from two towns in Arkansas.

Bonnie Tyler (Gaynor Hopkins)

Singer. Had hit single with "Total Eclipse of the Heart."

Rob Tyner (Robert Derminer)

Lead vocals of the Detroit band MC5 that produced creative youth-oriented rock in the 1960s.

Ritchie Valens (Ricardo Valenzuela)

Singer. Hits included "La Bamba" and "Donna."

Frankie Valli (Frank Castellucio)

Singer and member of The Four Seasons.

Dave Vanian (David Letts)

Rock star. Lead singer of The Damned.

Vanilla Ice (Robert van Winkle)

Rap artist. Most famous for his hit "Ice Ice Baby."

Bobby Vee (Robert Velline)

1950s rock star.

Tom Verlaine (Thomas Miller)

Lead guitar and vocals for the band Television.

Sid Vicious (John Simon Ritchie)

Rock star in group The Sex Pistols.

Sid Vicious allegedly took his stage name from Johnny Rotten's pet hamster.

Butch Vig (Brian Vig)

Producer for Nirvana and Smashing Pumpkins. Member of the band Garbage.

Gene Vincent (Vincent Eugene Craddock)

Lead singer of Gene and the Blue Caps in the 1950s.

Vitamin C (Colleen Fitzpatrick)

Pop singer.

Junior Walker (Autry DeWalt Walker Jr.)

Saxophonist.

Warren G (Warren Griffin III)

Rapper.

Dionne Warwick (Dionne Warrick)

Grammy award winning singer. Warwick participated in the celebrity AIDS benefit single, "That's what freinds are for."

Dionne Warwick's birth name was Marie Dionne Warrick, but on her first album in '62 her last name was misspelled Warwick, and she then adopted that spelling. For a brief period in the '70s, she changed the spelling of Warwick to Warwicke, based on advice from a numerologist. Finally, in the '80s she changed it back to Warwick.

Dave Was (David Weiss)

Producer, flutist, and featured orchestral soloist for *The Lion King*.

Don Was (Donald Fagenson)
Music producer.

Dinah Washington (Ruth Jones)
Blues, jazz, and gospel singer.

Muddy Waters (McKinley Morganfield)
One of the most famous artists of the 1930s and 1940s Chicago jazz scene.

Dean Ween (Mickey Melchiondo)
Punk rock star and member of Ween.

Gene Ween (Aaron Freeman)
Punk rock star and member of Ween.

> The band **Ween** used the punk surname tradition of The Ramones as an example, becoming Gene and Dene Ween, although they are not really brothers.

Paul Weller (John Weller)
British front man for The Jam and The Style Council, now in the middle of his solo career.

Kim Wilde (Kim Smith)
Sang "Kids in America."

Hank Williams (Hiram Williams)
Country-western artist.

Otis Williams (Otis Myers)
Singer and leader of Temptations.

Nicky Wire (Nicholas Jones)
Member of the band Manic Street Preachers.

Wish Bone (Charles Scruggs)
Hip-hop artist with group Bone Thugs-n-Harmony.

Stevie Wonder (Steveland Morris)
Pop artist.

Bill Wyman (William Perks)
Bassist for The Rolling Stones.

Tammy Wynette (Virginia Pugh)
Country-western artist.

Weird Al Yankovic (Alfred Matthew Yankovic)
Comedic singer-spoof.

WRITERS

WRITERS

ALIAS (REAL NAME)

Agate (Whitelaw Reid)
Newspaper reporter and editor of *The Washington Tribune*.
Member of Peace Commission for the Spanish-American War.

Sholem Aleichem (Sholem Rabinovich)
Author of short stories, dramatist, and humorist.

Ali Baba (Alberigh Mackay)
Taught classes at "The Rajkumar Class," which was the beginning
of Daly College.

Piers Anthony (Piers Anthony Dillingham Jacob)
Wrote books on many subjects, including martial arts, fantasy, and
science fiction.

Guillaume Apollinaire (Guillaume Albert Vladimir Apollinaire de Kostrowitzky)
Poet, writer, and art critic. Published novels, stories, and art
criticisms.

Michael Arlen (Dikran Kuyumjian)
English novelist.

Atlas (Edmund Yates)

Novelist.

David Axton (Dean Koontz)

Novelist. Latest work under this pen name is *The Taking*.

B B (Denys Watkins-Pitchford)

Taught art at Rugby School. Illustrated his own books.

Richard Bachman (Stephen King)

Novelist. King wrote *Thinner* under his pen name.

Stephen King released several novels, including *The Long Walk Home* and *Running Man* under the name of Richard Bachman to designate a different writing voice (he also wanted to see how well an unknown writer would do). King developed a thrilling account of a writer's relation to his pseudonymous self in the novel *The Dark Half*—a Cain and Abel-like story inspired by the King-Bachman relationship.

Ada S. Ballin (Mrs. Oscar G. D. Berry)

Author of *The Science of Dress*. Promoted the merits of wearing woolen clothing.

Lionel Bart (Lionel Begleiter)

Wrote the text for several musicals, but only *Oliver!*, for which he won a Tony was really successful.

Beachcomber (D.B. Wyndham-Lewis and John Bingham Morton)

Satirist. Wrote for a newspaper.

Acton Bell (Anne Bronte)

Remembered primarily as "the third Bronte sister." Wrote poetry.

Currer Bell (Charlotte Bronte)
Author of *Jane Eyre*.

Ellis Bell (Emily Bronte)
Probably the greatest writer of the Bronte sisters. Wrote *Wuthering Heights*.

John Beynon (John Wyndham Parkes Lucas Beynon Harris)
Author of *The Seeds of Time*.

Charlotte, Emily, and **Anne Brontë** published a book of poems under the male pseudonyms Currier, Ellis and Acton Bell. Readers at that time were more receptive to the voice of men, and controversial ideas could at least find an audience when women wrote under male pseudonyms.

George A. Birmingham (James Owen Hannay)
Novelist and vicar of Holy Trinity Church, Kensington.

Nicholas Blake (Cecil Day Lewis)
Poet, critic, and educator. Appointed Poet Laureate in 1968.

Nellie Bly (Elizabeth Cochrane Seaman)
Journalist who wrote about conditions in mental institutions.

Capt. Ralph Bonehill (Edward Stratemeyer)
Created fictional characters, such as The Hardy Boys, Nancy Drew, and The Bobbsey Twins.

Edgar Box (Gore Vidal)
Author of the novel *Williwaw*.

Boz (Charles Dickens)
Wrote A *Tale of Two Cities* and *Scrooge*.

Bessie Bramble (Elizabeth Wade)
Journalist, suffragette, and social worker.

James Bridie (Osborne Henry Mavor)
Founding father of modern Scottish theatre.

Anthony Burgess (John B. Wilson)
Novelist, composer, and critic.

Lewis Carroll (Rev. Charles Lutwidge Dodgson)
Author of *Alice in Wonderland*.

Leslie Charteris (Leslie Charles Bowyer Lin)
Author of *The Saint*.

Joseph Conrad (Jozef Teodor Konrad Nalecz Korzeniowski)
Author of *Heart of Darkness*.

Marie Corelli (Mary Mackay)
Author of *A Romance of Two Worlds*.

Baron Corvo (Frederick Rolfe)
Author of *Hadrian the Seventh*.

Christopher Crowfield (Harriet Beecher Stowe)
Author of *Uncle Tom's Cabin*.

Alan Dale (Alfred J. Cohen)
Writer, actor, and producer.

Frank Danby (Julia Frankau)

British novelist.

Gérard de Nerval (Gérard Labrunie)

His translation of *Faust* made him famous. He also wrote and translated poetry and short stories.

Dr. Seuss (Theodore Seuss Geisel)

Famous children's author.

It's said that **Theodor Geisel** got into trouble after a college drinking session and he started publishing under his mother's maiden name, Seuss, so he could keep writing for the school paper. Later, he added a distinguishing title in honor of his father, who'd wanted Theodor to become a doctor. Publishing companies turned down Geisel at least 30 times before he employed the pen name of Dr. Seuss, and thereafter enjoyed remarkable success.

Brian Eldred (Ray Bradbury)

One of Mr. Bradbury's many pseudonyms, he wrote *How to Run a Successful Ghost Agency* and *The Electrocution* under this name.

Elia (Charles Lamb)

Wrote *The Adventures of Ulysses*.

George Eliot (Mary Ann Evans)

Wrote *Silas Marner*.

Harlan Ellison (Ellis Hart)

Contemporary American short-story writer.

Paul Eluard (Eugène Grindel)

Poet and surrealist.

Fanny Fern (Sara P. Parton)
Newspaper columnist.

Ford Madox Ford (Ford Hermann Hueffer)
English writer and editor.

C. S. Forester (Cecil Lewis Troughton Smith)
Wrote the series *Horatio Hornblower*.

Francis Forrester (Daniel Wise)
Author of *My Uncle Toby's Library*.

Anatole France (Jacques Anatole François Thibault)
Novelist.

Christopher Fry (Christopher Harris)
Wrote *Ben-Hur*.

Lewis Grassie Gibbon (James Leslie Mitchell)
Scottish writer who lived only six years after becoming a professional writer, but managed to produce over seventeen full-length books in that time. Known for *Sunset Song*.

Maxim Gorky (Aleksei Maksimovich Peshkov)
Russian playwright, novelist, and political activist.

Henry Green (Henry Vincent Yorke)
Novelist.

Barton Grey (George Herbert Sass)
Novelist and short-story writer.

H.D. (Hilda Doolittle)

Poet and novelist.

Steffie Hall (Janet Evanovich)

Author of the Stephanie Plum series that includes *One for the Money* and *Two for the Dough*. Wrote some books under the pen name Steffie Hall.

Knut Hamsun (Knut Pederson)

Novelist and poet.

Frances Harrod (Frances Forbes-Robertson)

Novelist and painter.

Alice Hawthorne (Septimus Winner)

Pop music star.

O. Henry (William Sydney Porter)

Author of *Gift of the Magi*.

Herblock (Herbert L. Block)

Pulitzer-Prize winning cartoonist and political humorist.

James Herriot (James Alfred Wight)

Author and veterinarian.

Patricia, Claire Highsmith, Morgan (Mary Patricia Plangman)

James Alfred Wight published stories of creatures great and small under the name James Herriot.

American mystery writer whose works were especially successful in Europe.

Evan Hunter (Salvatore Lombino)

A.k.a. Ed McBain. Salvatore wrote *The Blackboard Jungle* under the Evan Hunter pen name.

Michael Innes (J. I. M. Stewart)

Novelist, educator, and scholar.

Ivory Black (Thomas A. Janvier)

Wrote about life in New York City during the 19th century.

Joseph Kell (Anthony Burgess Wilson)

Author of *A Clockwork Orange*.

Marie Kelvedon (Sarah Kane)

British playwright.

As a book reviewer for the *Yorkshire Post*, **Anthony Burgess Wilson**, author of *A Clockwork Orange*, once gave a scathing review to one of his own novels, originally published under the name of Joseph Kell.

Dietrich Knickerbocker (Washington Irving)

Author, short story writer, and poet. Had other pen names as well.

Anne Knish (Arthur Davison Ficke)

Poet.

John le Carré (David Cornwell)

British novelist.

Stan Lee (Stanley Martin Lieber)

Creator of Marvel Comic classics such as *Spider-Man*.

Murray Leinster (William Fitzgerald Jenkins)

Author of *Time Tunnel*.

Hugh MacDiarmid (Christopher Murray Grieve)

Scottish writer, poet, novelist, and essayist.

Ed McBain (Salvatore Lombino)

A.k.a. Evan Hunter. Salvatore wrote police procedurals, including the *87th Precinct* series, under the Evan Hunter pen name.

Catherine Marchant (Catherine Cookson)

Author of *A Mystical Unicorn*.

Marilyn (Peter Robinson)

Novelist.

Andre Maurois (Emile Herzog)

Biographer.

Barbara Michaels (Barbara Mertz)

Novelist and mystery writer.

Finn Mickey (Ernest Jarrold)

Novelist.

Margaret Mitchell (Peggy Marsh)

Author of *Gone With the Wind*.

> **Peggy Marsh** grew up to write the classic novel *Gone With the Wind*. The shy Marsh wrote under the name of Margaret Mitchell.

Molière (Jean Baptiste Poquelin)

French poet.

Alberto Moravia (Alberto Pincherle)

Novelist.

Emanuel Morgan (Witter Bynner)

Poet.

Geoffrey Mortimer (Walter M. Gallichan)

Author.

Pablo Neruda (Ricardo Eliezer Neftali Reyes)

Famous Chilean poet known for his moving Spanish love poetry and startling imagery.

Pablo Neruda used his pen name after Czech writer and poet Jan Neruda to avoid conflict with his parents because they did not want him to become an author. It would later become his legal name.

E. Nesbit (Mrs. Hubert Bland)

Poet and author of children's literature.

Danbury Newsman (J. M. Bailey)

Humorist and editor.

Leigh Nichols (Dean Koontz)

A contemporary writer of strange, compelling novels that are sometimes classified as sci-fi and sometimes as thrillers.

Bill Nye (Edgar Wilson Nye)

Humorist and journalist.

Flann O'Brien (Brian O'Nolan)

Novelist.

Frank O'Connor (Michael O'Donovan)

Irish author who wrote short stories, screenplays, and novels, such as *My Oedipus Complex.*

Ruth Ogden (Frances Otis Ide)

Novelist.

George Orwell (Eric Arthur Blair)

Author.

Ouida (Marie Louise de la Ramée)

English novelist.

Palinurus (Cyril Connolly)

English critic and editor.

Parson Lot (Charles Kingsley)

English author and clergyman.

Elizabeth Peters (Barbara Mertz)

Mystery writer.

Ellis Peters (Edith Pargeter)

Mystery writer.

Jean Plaidy (Eleanor Hibbert)

British writer.

Poor Richard (Benjamin Franklin)

Author of *Poor Richard's Almanac.*

Benjamin Franklin wrote *Poor Richard's Almanac* under the pseudonym of Richard Saunders, a poor man who needed money to care for his family.

Dorothy Prescott (Agnes Blake Poor)

Novelist.

Publius (Alexander Hamilton, James Madison, and John Jay)

Name under which they wrote *The Federalist Papers*.

Q (Arthur Quiller-Couch)

Novelist.

Ellery Queen (Manfred Lee and his cousin Frederic Dannay)

Authors of *Ellery Queen* mysteries.

Dan Quinn (Alfred Henry Lewis)

Journalist and novelist.

Walter Ramal (Walter de la Mare)

Poet.

Anne Rampling (Howard Allen O'Brien)

A.k.a. Anne Rice. Wrote *Exit to Eden* and *Belinda* under this pen name.

Pauline Réage (Dominique Aury)

Novelist.

John Reid (Andrew Tobias)

Tobias published *The Best Little Boy in the World* under the pen name John Reid due to fear of his parents' reaction. The classic coming-of-age story was first released in 1973, and has since been re-issued, identifying the real name of its author.

Mary Renault (Eileen Mary Challans)

Novelist.

Sax Rhomer (Arthur Sarsfield Ward)

Author of *Fu Manchu* stories.

Jean Rhys (Ellen Gwendolen Rees Williams)

Female author who dealt with the experience of a woman victimized by her dependence on a European male. Best known for her novel *Wide Sargasso Sea*.

Anne Rice (Howard Allen O'Brien)

Author of *Interview with the Vampire*. Also known as Anne Rampling.

Anne Rice has at least 2 pseudonyms. One is Anne Rampling. *The Claiming of Sleeping Beauty, Beauty's Punishment*, and *Beauty's Release*, are erotic novels she wrote under the pseudonym of A. N. Roquelaure.

J. D. Robb (Nora Roberts)

Roberts uses the Robb pen name for her *In Death* mystery series.

A. Mary F. Robinson (Madame Emile Duclaux)

Poet.

Jules Romains (Louis-Henri-Jean Farigoule)

French novelist, dramatist, and poet. Founder of the literary movement known as Unanimisme.

A. N. Roquelaure (Howard Allen O'Brien)

A.k.a. Anne Rice. Wrote soft-porn novels under this pen name.

Adrian Ross (Arthur Reed Ropes)

Author of *On the Bridge*.

Salman Rushdie (Ahmed Rushdie)

Author of *Satanic Verses*.

Francoise Sagan (Francoise Quoires)

French authoress, who wrote novels detailing the romantic lives of young women having affairs. One of the first celebrity authors of the 1970s.

Saki (Hector Hugh Munro)

Scottish author who wrote satire about the Edwardian social scene.

George Sand (Amandine Aurore Dupin Lucie)

French author who wrote about women's rights.

John Sandford (John Roswell Camp)

Author of the *Prey* series.

Nevil Shute (Nevil Shute Norway)

Popular novelist.

Colette Sidonie (Gabrielle Colette)

Novelist.

Ignazio Silone (Secondo Tranquilli)

Author of Fontamara, one of the most influential, and earliest, "realistic" novels about fascism.

Vladimir Sirin (Vladimir Navokov)

Novelist.

Cordwainer Smith (Paul Myron Anthony Linebarger)

Science fiction writer.

Rosamond Smith (Joyce Carol Oates)

Very prolific writer. Her most popular work is probably *We Were the Mulvaneys*, but she also wrote *Man Crazy, Broke Heart Blues,* and *Double Delight.*

Stevie Smith (Florence Margaret Smith)

Famed poetess and author. Her most famous work is her poem "Not Waving but Drowning."

Lemony Snicket (Daniel Handler)

Author of a series of children's books known as *A Series of Unfortunate Events.*

Leonard Spaulding (Ray Bradbury)

One of Mr. Bradbury's many pseudonyms, he wrote *The Highway* under this name.

Alice Spinner (Mrs. Augusta Zelia Fraser)

Novelist.

Burt L. Standish (Gilbert Pattern)

Novelist.

Stendhal (Marie-Henri Beyle)

Novelist.

Italo Svevo (Ettore Schmitz)

Novelist.

James Jr. Tiptree (Alice Sheldon)
Author of science fiction.

Tivoli (Horace W. Bleackley)
Author of *Life of John Wilkes*.

Mark Twain (Samuel Langhorne Clemens)
Successful journalist and humorist. Author of many classic American novels, such as *Tom Sawyer* and *The Adventures of Huckleberry Finn*.

Samuel Langhorne Clemens started using the pen name of Mark Twain after training as a riverboat pilot on the Mississippi. "Mark twain" was a phrase that boatmen used to indicate two fathoms of water (or 12 feet), the depth needed for a boat's safe passage along the river. But Clemens was always careful to distinguish himself from Twain. While people found Clemens to be a narcissist and emotionally unstable, Twain was described as charming, generous and funny.

Uncle Remus (Joel Chandler Harris)
Famous for his "Br'er Rabbit" tales.

Babara Vine (Ruth Rendell)
Novelist.

Voltaire (François-Marie Arouet)
French social satirist.

Artemus Ward (Charles Farrar Browne)
Wrote humorous works.

Dame Rebecca West (Cicily Isabel Fairfield)

English journalist, novelist, and critic. West is perhaps best known for her reports on the Nuremberg trials (1945-46). Her companion for 10 years was H. G. Wells.

Nathanael West (Nathan Wallenstein Weinstein)

American writer whose most famous novel, Miss Lonelyhearts, rose to popularity after his premature death. Wrote about the sterility and materialism of the American Dream.

Mary Westmacott (Dame Agatha Clarissa Mary Christie)

English author of detective stories.

Oscar Wilde (Sebastian Melmouth)

Playwright, sharp social critic.

Tennessee Williams (Thomas Lanier Williams)

Playwright.

OTHER FAMOUS PEOPLE

OTHER FAMOUS PEOPLE

Below are people who are famous for reasons other than acting, singing, or writing. These include political figures, teachers, inventors, and outlaws.

ALIAS (REAL NAME)

Paddy Ashdown (Jeremy John Durham Ashdown)
British politician. Leader of the Liberal Democrats from 1988 to 1999.

Kemal Ataturk (Mustapha Kemal)
National Hero and First President of the New Turkish Republic.

Ayatollah Khomeini (Ruhollah Hendi)
Founder of the Islamic Republic of Iran.

Billy the Kid (Henry McCarty, William H. Bonney)
Outlaw.

Nicolas Bourbaki (Various)
A group of 20th-century mathematicians who wrote a series of treatises on pure mathematics.

Willy Brandt (Herbert Ernst Karl Frahm)

Fourth Federal Chancellor of the Federal Republic of Germany, member of European Parliament.

Donnie Brasco (Joe Pistone)

FBI agent Mafia infiltrator.

Buffalo Bill (William Frederick Cody)

Adventurer.

> After **Joe Pistone** brought down the Bonanno family, he went into the Witness Protection Program with a new identity. To this day, there is a contract on his life.

Jean Cacharel (Louis Henri Bousquet)

Fashion designer.

Ali Campbell (Alastair Campbell)

Former communications chief for the Prime Minister of Britain.

Robert Capa (Andre Friedman)

Famed photographer in World War II.

Carlos "The Jackal" (Ramirez Sanchez)

Terrorist and professional revolutionary.

Butch Cassidy (George Robert LeRoy Parker)

Outlaw.

Coco Chanel (Gabrielle Bonheur Chanel)

Fashion designer.

Dalai Lama (Tenzin Gyatso)

14th Dalai Lama.

> **Dalai** means "ocean" in Mongolian and Lama is Tibetan for "spiritual teacher."

Gerald Ford (Leslie Lynch King)
38th President of the United States.

Mahatma Gandhi (Mohandas Karamchand Gandhi)
Indian proponent of "non-violence" in ending India's colonial status in the British empire.

Samuel Goldwyn (Samuel Gelbfisz)
Film producer and founder of MGM.

H.A.L. 2000 (Heuristically ALgorythmic model 2000)
Computer.

> Some conspiracy theorists link **H.A.L.** with IBM due to each letter following each other in order (H I, A B, L M).

Chiang Kai-Shek (Jiang Jie Shi)
First president of Taiwan.

Gary Kasparov (Garri Weinstein)
Chess champion who claimed the title of world champion at 22.

Ann Landers (Esther Pauline Friedman)
Advice column writer.

> Ann Landers' sister Pauline Ester Friedman was better-known as Abby, as in "Dear Abby."

Lord Lucan (Richard John Bingham)
The "missing" 7th Earl of Lucan, suspected of murdering his children's nanny in 1974, and attempting to kill his estranged wife as well. Disappeared and has never been seen again.

Makarios III (Mikhail Khristodolou Mouskos)

Archbishop and primate for the autocephalous Cypriot Orthodox Church from 1950 to his death, president of Cyprus from 1959 to his death except for a short time in 1974 when he was removed by a coup.

Malcolm X (Malcolm Little)

Civil rights activist who advocated a less peaceful movement than his contemporary, Dr. Martin Luther King Jr.

Mata Hari (Margarete Gertrude Zelle)

Famous exotic dancer who was accused by the French, for whom she was spying, of being a double agent for the Germans during World War I.

Robert Maxwell (Jan Ludvik Hoch)

Originally born in Czechoslovakia, he moved to the UK and was eventually elected to the Parliament and later to a union. His questionable business ventures in publishing brought him public censure, and he died a questionable death at sea.

Golda Meir (Golda Mabovitch)

Campaigned for the creation of the nation of Israel, later became a leading politician and stateswoman for the new country.

Mother Teresa (Agnes Gonxha Bojaxhiu)

Indian nun who was known for her work with the poor and destitute. Won the Nobel Peace Prize in 1979, and was awarded sainthood after her death in 1997.

Mother Teresa took her name in honor of Teresa of Avila and Therese de Lisiex.

Kwame Nkrumah (Francis Nuria Kofi)

"Father of African Nationalism," former Prime Minister of Ghana.

U Nu (Thankin Nu)

Won the first general election in Burma but was overthrown in a military coup two years later.

Shimon Peres (Shimon Persky)

Originally Polish, he became one of Israel's most influential leaders holding posts in foreign ministry as well as internal affairs.

Pope John Paul II (Karl Josef Wojtyla)

First non-Italian to be chosen Pope in over 400 years.

Pope John XXIII (Angelo Giuseppe Roncalli)

Elected Pope in 1958.

Pope Paul VI (Giovanni Battista Montini)

Wrote encyclical Humanae Vitae/Of Human Life (1968).

Pope Pius XII (Eugenio Pacelli)

Only Pope to proclaim papal infallibility.

Pol Pot (Saloth Sar)

Leader of the Khmer Rouge, the Cambodian Communist insurgency movement, which is responsible for the genocide of up to 3 million people in Cambodia.

Yitzhak Shamir (Yitzhak Jazernicki)

Israeli Prime Minister until 1992.

Alan Smithee (Various)

Name used by directors who disown their own movie. Alan Smithee is the only name the Directors Guild of America allows for these directors. It is an anagram of "The Alias Men."

Joseph Stalin (Joseph Vissarionovitch Dzhugashvili)

Stalin (Russian from stal, meaning "steel") was originally a nickname for Joseph, but it stuck, so he continued to use it.

Russian dictator during World War II.

Leopold Anthony Stokowski (Antoni Stanislaw Boleslawawich)

Celebrated British-born American composer and conductor known for his work with the Philadelphia Orchestra.

Student (William Sealey Gosset)

Discoverer of the t-distribution in statistics.

Kim Il Sung (Kim Song Ju)

Professional Korean Revolutionary during the Japanese occupation.

Leon Trotsky (Lev Bronstein)

Contemporary of Lenin, one of the leaders of Communist Russia, and creator of the Red Army.

Mao Tse-tung (Mao Ze Dong)

Leader of the Chinese Communist party from 1935. Brought the party into power, and unified a China mostly free of foreign domination for the first time since the Opium Wars.

Sun Yat-sen (Sun Zhong Shan)

Recognized by Chinese everywhere as their country's modern founder, the physician-turned-nationalist failed in his dream of unification.